COOK – AND ENJOY IT

How often do you say, 'It isn't worth cooking a meal for only one or two.'

This book sets out to change your mind. There are many who live alone or with just one other person who feel that a proper meal is not worth the trouble. But it is; and whether you want starters, main course or sweets this little book is full of straightforward yet interesting dishes. There is nothing that needs elaborate preparation, nor are the recipes full of rare and expensive ingredients. There are shopping hints to follow so that you won't finish up with a mass of half-used ingredients. And if you do cook for large numbers there are simple guidelines to help you cope.

To Jonathan

ACKNOWLEDGEMENTS

I would like to thank Patty Fisher for supplying the calorie and food values charts, Christine Campbell, Jim Woods and my brother-in-law Daniel Brostoff for all their help and advice, and Madeleine White for many hours of typing. Without Bill Kolins none of this would have been possible.

Cook—
and enjoy it

Deanna Brostoff

CORONET BOOKS
Hodder and Stoughton

Printed and bound in Great Britain for
Coronet Books, Hodder and Stoughton,
St. Paul's House, Warwick Lane,
London, EC4P 4AH
by Hunt Barnard Printing Ltd,
Aylesbury, Bucks.

ISBN 0 340 19856 7

Contents

Introduction

I have always had a great love for food and cooking, but when I lived alone even I was daunted by the prospect of preparing any of the dishes presented in those mammoth glossy cookery books. I used to sit munching my cheese on toast staring at the mouth-watering pictures in my cookbooks. It wasn't only the lengthy preparations involved for cooking such a small amount that put me off, but also the sheer economics involved. I couldn't afford the long lists of ingredients which, partially used, would lie like white elephants in my little store cupboard. So many of the recipes also demanded a wide variety of kitchen equipment and, in all honesty, it seemed silly to buy, for example, a range of baking tins, piping bags or a food mixer when I would hardly ever use them.

When I started to cook for a living I decided to write a book that would help people who, like myself, lived alone but wanted to eat well and economically. I hope you will read the chapter on shopping tips before you venture out and, if you can only manage to shop once a week, have a look at the Cookery Calendar. Here are ideas for meals for a month, bearing in mind as much as possible that what is left over from one day can often be used up cold or as an ingredient for what you eat the next. As far as kitchen equipment goes, there are, of course, essentials which you should have that can be used as multi-purpose cooking dishes – I have mentioned these throughout the book.

I am now cooking for two – I have a hungry husband who was delighted to put his seal of approval on these recipes for me. I hope this book will help people like myself who want to cook and enjoy it.

1 A General Guide

SHOPPING TIPS

1. MAKE OUT A SHOPPING LIST. This is probably the most important shopping tip as a list will save you time, money and effort. Sit down with a paper and pencil and think about what you'll be eating over the next few days – main meals, snacks, fruit, breakfasts. Read the recipe ingredients in this book carefully when making your list and remember to check your store cupboard for the 'basics' – tea, coffee, sugar, etc. You will then have an approximate idea of how much you'll be spending before you leave home.

2. LOOK OUT FOR BARGAINS. Take advantage of Special Offers and 'Super Saves', they offer worthwhile savings. Supermarkets sell canned foods under their own labels – these are good quality and cheaper than brand-name products. (They're often made by the same firms as the brand-name products for sale under the supermarket label.) Keep an eye open in supermarkets for dented and battered cans which are reduced simply because of their appearance – the contents are fine.

3. THINK ABOUT BUYING BIG. Even if you are only cooking for one you should consider buying the *large* jar of coffee, the *large* cooking oil and, in fact, the large size of anything non-perishable that you use constantly – household items too, detergents, washing-up liquid, etc. This is far more economical in the long run – work it out for yourself next time you go shopping. There is, of course, a double saving if the large size is on 'Special Offer'.

4. SAVE ANY COUPONS that drop through the letterbox offering 'Money Off' soap powders, coffee, etc., even if you don't use the product. Take the coupons with you when you go shopping and you'll find that most supermarkets will accept these coupons as part payment of your shopping without your having to purchase the product, as long as the supermarket stocks the 'Money Off' product.

5. NEVER SHOP WHEN YOU'RE HUNGRY because it leads to impulse buying. Besides being expensive, you're quite likely to clutter your shelves with all those things (exotic sardines, fancy soups) which will always seem too costly or too mysterious to open. Buy only what is on your list. The less time spent shopping, the less money spent.

6. DON'T FEEL SHY about asking for the single chop or $\frac{1}{4}$ lb mince. Lots of single shoppers buy more perishable food than they want because they're too embarassed to ask for a small amount or to find out if smaller portions are available. It's worth getting to know the local shops, the small ones and the supermarkets, cultivating friendly assistants and asking their advice. A number of supermarkets prepare and pack the meat at the back of the shops, so if you can't find what you want in the cabinet ask an assistant. Sainsbury's provide special telephones at their meat cabinets for customers to use. Pick up the phone, ask for what you want and it will be with you in minutes.

7. LOOK AT WHAT YOU'RE BUYING and at what you're getting for your money. Stop and compare sizes and prices. Make sure you're buying sound fruit, good vegetables, fresh bread. Look for cheaper cuts of meats and bacon – you will often find 'second cut' rashers which don't quite qualify for the 'prime' label, and streaky bacon is always cheaper than prime back. If you always eat the same foods, look around and try something different which is the same price – a new sort of cheese or pasta, a different cut of meat. You can vary your food enormously without spending more money.

8. FOR YOUR OWN COMFORT try, if possible, to shop at the less crowded times of the week. Fridays and Saturdays are always busy (if you shop then, shop early) and so are lunch times.

THE COOKERY CALENDAR

This is the point where you can stop saying 'What on earth shall I eat today?' The Cookery Calendar gives you ideas and shopping lists for a month of main meals. There is a different suggestion for each day and each day's shopping is on a separate list, so you can easily change the dishes around. There is, of course, no reason at all why your week should start on the Monday – it just made it simpler to compile the calendar – but remember that Sunday's shopping is always listed for the Saturday. I have suggested vegetables or puddings on some days, but these are *not* included in the shopping lists.

THE BASIC KITCHEN STAPLES

You will probably have most of these 'basics' in your store cupboard already. I have listed the 'basics' required for each day's main meal under the shopping list to remind you to check your stores.

Margarine	Pepper, black and/or
Cooking oil or fat	white
Brown sugar	Vinegar, ordinary malt
White sugar	Rice
Flour	Stock cubes, beef and
Salt	chicken

Lemon juice – a squeezy
  Jif is handy when you
  need some lemon juice
Dried breadcrumbs,
  bought or homemade
Dried mixed herbs
Dried sage
Dried bay leaves
Ground ginger
Mixed spice
Tomato ketchup
Cornflour
Mustard powder
Tomato purée – a tube
  lasts ages
Dried onion

WEEK I	MONDAY	TUESDAY	WEDNESDAY
	Chicken with Orange Casserole (p. 88)	Hot Tongue (p. 125)	Spaghetti with Tomato, Bacon and Pepper Sauce (p. 166-7)
NOTES	Save the bacon rinds to flavour tomorrow's tongue Grate the rind of the remaining ½ orange and add with the juice to mashed potatoes for a new and delicious taste	2 tongues are ample for one meal, but you might like to cook extra to serve in a different way tomorrow (pp. 125–127) Cold tongue keeps happily for 4–5 days in a refrigerator	If green peppers are unavailable or too expensive, add the bacon to the plain tomato sauce and serve with grated cheese
SHOPPING LIST	1–2 chicken pieces 2 bacon rashers 1 orange	2–4 fresh lambs' tongues	1 pkt. spaghetti or macaroni 1 small can tomatoes 1 small green pepper 2–3 bacon rashers
STORE CUPBOARD CHECK	Flour Margarine ½ teaspoon dried onion Chicken stock cube Bay leaf	Chicken or beef stock cube Bay leaf	

THURSDAY	FRIDAY	SATURDAY	SUNDAY
Sausage Supper (p. 123)	Soused Herring (p. 135)	Cauliflower Cheese (p. 153)	Baked Glazed Bacon (p. 118)
Extra sausages can be cooked tomorrow and served with eggs	This is equally tasty hot or cold. Serve with a crusty roll and boiled potatoes or a potato salad Buy a large onion as the rest will be used to cook Sunday's bacon joint	Use any extra uncooked cauliflower to make a salad tomorrow (p. 158) N.B. Don't forget to soak tomorrow's bacon in cold water overnight	There will be enough bacon for a cold meal tomorrow – or make a risotto
1 small pkt. sausages 1 egg 1 pkt. mashed potatoes	1–2 herrings, boned and filleted 1 large onion Peppercorns	Bread for fresh breadcrumbs 1 cauliflower 1 pkt. cheese sauce mix Piece of cheese – you'll want to grate some 1 small smoked bacon forehock joint (1–1½ lbs) 1 carrot	
Flour Margarine	Bay leaf Vinegar	Bay leaf Brown sugar	

WEEK 2	MONDAY	TUESDAY	WEDNESDAY
	Liver with Lemon and Herbs (p. 114)	Baked Stuffed Onion (p. 149)	Chicken Maryland (p. 90)
NOTES	The recipe suggests serving the liver in a ring of savoury rice – you could have plain rice or mashed potato	A green salad would be a nice accompaniment You may have grated or hard cheese left over from Saturday. See notes on storing grated cheese on p. 23	Serve with hot sweetcorn or sweetcorn fritters
SHOPPING LIST	3 oz pig's liver or lamb's liver 1 small lemon	1 large onion 3 slices ham, bacon or ham loaf Bread Cheese	1–2 chicken pieces 1 egg 1 banana
STORE CUPBOARD CHECK	Cornflour Sugar Mixed herbs Cooking oil	Dried sage Margarine	2–3 tablespoons dried bread-crumbs Flour Cooking oil or fat

THURSDAY	FRIDAY	SATURDAY	SUNDAY
Ham Steak with Grilled Apple Rings (p. 106)	Baked Fish with Cheese Crumble (p. 130)	Spare Ribs with Sweet and Sour Sauce (p. 77)	Braised Beef in Beer (p. 59)
If you buy a packet of 2 ham steaks and only use one, serve the other tomorrow with a fried egg on top	Why not bake a pudding at the same time? If you are out of cheese, add it to the shopping list	1–2 spare ribs can be kept aside and used as part of a Sunday brunch mixed grill tomorrow Have a look at the chapter on Baking – you might like to bake a tea loaf for the weekend. Nice to eat in the week too!	Bake a jacket potato and/or a pudding at the same time
ham steak apple	1 cod or haddock steak	¾–1 lb pork spare ribs 1 small can pineapple slices ½–1 lb stewing steak 1 onion 1 large potato Bread 1 bottle Pale or Brown Ale	
brown sugar	Lemon juice Grated cheese Margarine	Mustard powder Vinegar Lemon juice Brown sugar Tomato ketchup Ground ginger Flour Cornflour Margarine	

WEEK 3	MONDAY	TUESDAY	WEDNESDAY
	Devilled Turkey Drumsticks (p. 100)	Mixed Vegetable Pie (p. 154)	Continental Kidneys (p. 112)
NOTES	Any leftovers are very tasty cold If you can't get turkey drumsticks – use chicken ones! Serve with hot macaroni – cook a little extra and leave in a bowl of cold water for tomorrow	As you will see from the recipe, all sorts of things can be added to this pie – so have a look in the store cupboard	Grate the kidney fat and store in a screw-top jar. Use whenever you nee suet, e.g. the Bacon Pudding on Friday Pour any remainin sour cream or yogurt over chopped fresh fruit. Sprinkle with brown sugar
SHOPPING LIST	1–2 turkey drumsticks Chutney Bread for fresh breadcrumbs	8 oz mixed vegetables fresh, canned or frozen 1 packet cheese sauce mix Peas	2 lamb's kidneys 1 small onion 2 oz mushrooms 1 carton natural yoghurt or sour cream
STORE CUPBOARD CHECK	Tomato ketchup Mustard powder Mixed spice Margarine	Grated cheese Milk to make up cheese sauce mix Breadcrumbs Macaroni	Margarine Flour Beef stock cube Tomato puree Macaroni or rice

THURSDAY	FRIDAY	SATURDAY	SUNDAY
Smoked Haddock with Poached Eggs (p. 142)	Bacon Pudding (p. 120)	Lamb Chop in pastry (p. 71)	Spiced Chicken and Apricots (p. 90)
If you prefer use smoked cod or whiting	Tasty served with fresh or canned fried tomatoes	Serve with green vegetables	Serve with green salad and plain boiled rice Use the extra apricots for a pudding tomorrow
1–2 pieces smoked haddock 2 eggs	2–3 rashers streaky bacon 1 small onion 1 egg	1 lamb chop 1–2 chicken pieces 1 onion A 15-oz can apricot halves Curry powder	
Margarine Milk for poaching fish	Self-raising flour Mustard powder 1 oz suet or kidney fat	Self-raising flour $\frac{1}{2}$ oz suet or kidney fat Cooking oil Lemon juice $\frac{1}{4}$ chicken stock cube	

WEEK 4	MONDAY	TUESDAY	WEDNESDAY
	Stuffed Cabbage Leaves (p. 150)	Bacon Chop with Pineapple Rice (p. 79)	Chicken in a Pot (p. 91)
NOTES	Extra uncooked mince can be used in lots of ways – e.g. Sage and Onion Mince, Hamburger, Meat Loaf – but you *must* use it next day (recipes in 'More Meat Meals'. Chap. 5)	Save extra pineapple for a pudding tomorrow with custard	Why not have a ho grilled grapefruit to begin the meal? (p. 173)
SHOPPING LIST	½ white cabbage ¼ lb minced beef	1 small can pineapple rings or pieces 1 bacon chop	1 pkt, mashed potato 2 carrots 1 onion 2 bacon rashers 1–2 chicken pieces
STORE CUPBOARD CHECK	Dried onion Rice ½ stock cube Tomato purée or ketchup Bay leaf	Brown sugar Vinegar Rice Butter	Margarine Dried mixed herbs Bay leaf Grated cheese

THURSDAY	FRIDAY	SATURDAY	SUNDAY
ork and Apple arcel (p. 76)	Baked Cod in Tomato Sauce (p. 132)	Liver, Bacon and Onion Casserole (p. 60)	Roast Lamb with Parsnips (p. 115)
ook 1–2 small otatoes at the me time oak a few prunes the juice of the tra ½ orange to t tomorrow n extra baking ple makes a per pudding ter in the week	Serve with hot buttered toast	Serve fruit and cheese afterwards	An ideal small roasting joint, giving you a hot and a cold meal If you don't like parsnips – roast swede or potatoes with the meat
pork chop small cooking apple orange	1 small can tomatoes 1 onion 1 cod cutlet	4 oz pig's liver 1 onion 3 rashers streaky bacon 1 best end of neck of lamb 2 parsnips	
oking oil ied sage tchen foil	Dried mixed herbs Margarine	Flour Cooking oil ¼ beef stock cube	

RECIPE HINTS

These hints and tips will, I hope, make the recipes even easier and provide some helpful short cuts.

1. Seasoned flour

In several of the recipes 'seasoned' flour is used to coat meat and fish. The seasoning adds extra flavour – simply add ½ teaspoon salt and ¼ level teaspoon pepper to each level tablespoon of flour, plain or self-raising. Ready-mixed seasoned flour can be kept in the store cupboard in a screw-top jar.

2. Paper bags

Save some paper bags as they will come in useful for coating food with flour or breadcrumbs. Put the flour or bread-crumbs in the bag, add the food and shake well. It saves crumbs going all over the floor. Paper bags also come in handy if you want to dry vegetables. Put any celery tops, spring onion tops, carrot and onion rings and parsley in a paper bag with holes in it. Fold over the top of the bag and leave them until completely dry. These dried vegetables are ideal for adding to soups and casseroles.

3. Breadcrumbs

To make dried breadcrumbs, Grate stale bread on a coarse grater, or use a liquidiser or coffee grinder. If you want the breadcrumbs to keep, melt 1 oz margarine in a pan, stir in 2 breakfast cups of coarse crumbs and dry off on a baking tray in the oven (when it is cooling down). Store for up to 2 months in an airtight jar.

If at any time you need breadcrumbs and you've no bread handy, crush some breakfast cereal with a rolling pin (put the cereal in a paper bag first).

4. Mushrooms

There is no need to peel cultivated mushrooms; just rinse them under running water and dry them with a cloth or on kitchen paper. Leave the mushrooms in their sealed punnet or, if bought loose, put them in an airtight kitchen container and store in the refrigerator or a cool larder. If fresh when bought, they will keep for 2–3 days in a good condition, but at the first signs of shrinking and wrinkling they should be used quickly. An egg slicer can be used to slice mushrooms.

5. Tomatoes

To skin tomatoes, cover them with boiling water, leave for a minute, drain and place in cold water. The skin will then slip off easily.

6. Pepper

There are two kinds of pepper, black and white. The white has a mild flavour and the black is more pungent. It's worth buying a small pepper mill if you enjoy the flavour of freshly ground black pepper. When whole peppercorns are called for in recipes, they will give more flavour if they are crushed beforehand with the back of a knife.

7. Hard-boiled Eggs

Always plunge hard-boiled eggs into cold water immediately they are cooked (12–15 minutes in simmering water). The cold water stops dark circles from forming round the yolks.

8. Cheese and Cheese Sauce

Any left-over bits of stale, hard cheese should be grated and kept in an airtight container in the refrigerator or a cool larder. Cheese can be kept in this way for up to 3 weeks in the refrigerator. Grated cheese comes in very handy for omelette fillings, snacks, stuffings, sauces, savoury crumbles, casserole toppings, baked potatoes, etc. – you'll find that lots of recipes in the book welcome a tablespoon or two of grated cheese!

Several recipes call for cheese sauce and, although there are many reliable sauce mixes to be bought, you may prefer to make your own, especially if you have the grated cheese on hand.

Homemade Cheese Sauce

Melt $\frac{1}{2}$ oz (1 level tablespoon) soft margarine in a pan, stir in 1 slightly rounded tablespoon flour, pour on $\frac{1}{4}$ pint milk and bring to the boil, stirring all the time. Cook for 2–3 minutes, remove from the heat and add 2–3 tablespoons grated cheese and a pinch of mustard powder. Stir until the cheese has melted.

If you use a sauce mix, you will probably only need half a packet. Store the rest in a screw-top jar in a cool dry place.

9. Onions

If you only need half an onion for a recipe, cut the onion in half before peeling it, wrap the unwanted half in foil and leave in a cool place. Ready-chopped onion can be stored overnight in the refrigerator or cool larder, but make sure that it's tightly wrapped in foil or put in a screw-top jar or sealed kitchen container to stop the smell spreading.

For any recipe that calls for 'finely chopped' onion, use a grater.

A packet of dried sliced onions is a very useful standby to have in the larder.

Shiny brown onion skins can be saved and added to meat soups and casseroles – they give colour and a rich flavour.

10. Too Salty!

Add a whole peeled raw potato to an over-salty soup or stew and cook for a few minutes – the potato will absorb the extra salt.

11. Herbs

Different herbs add interest and flavour to your cooking. Fresh herbs look charming and are easy to grow in small pots on a sunny window ledge. Buy dried herbs in the smallest amounts possible, store them in a cool dark place and don't keep them for too long or they will smell and taste musty. Remember that dried herbs are three times as strong as fresh herbs, so they should be used sparingly; and if a recipe calls for a 'pinch', don't feel tempted to add a teaspoon.

The herbs most frequently used in the recipes are bay leaves, thyme, parsley, sage and 'mixed herbs' – the last is a blend of marjoram, sage, parsley and thyme bought ready-mixed. Parsley stays fresh for several weeks if you put it in a polythene bag with a little water. Secure the bag firmly and store in the bottom of the refrigerator.

12. Reheating Foods

If you save food from one meal to be reheated for a meal on the following day, remember to cool the food as rapidly as you can after it is first cooked; cover and store in as cool a place as possible and then make sure you reheat it *thoroughly* next day. Food which is part cooked and left to cool slowly and then 'warmed' again rather than heated through thoroughly can be the cause of serious illness. If you are 'warming up' food, be sure it is *well heated right through*. Bring all soups and stews to the boil and then boil thoroughly for 5 minutes.

PENNY PINCHERS

1. To crisp up stale bread or rolls, sprinkle the tops with cold water and heat in a hot oven for 10 minutes or place in a thick, tightly closed saucepan over a low heat for 10 minutes, cool in the pan and then remove the lid.

2. Why boil a full kettle for two cuppas? Measure into the kettle the exact amount of water you need, making sure that the element is covered if you are using an electric kettle.

3. Save bacon rinds to flavour stews and stocks. They are also very tasty if crisply fried and sprinkled over soup or stews. (Fry on a high heat without any extra fat.)

4. You'll get more juice from lemons and oranges if you pour boiling water over them or pop them in a warm oven and leave for a few minutes.

5. Never throw away a squeezy bottle of detergent without first rinsing it out with warm water – you'll find there are enough suds for another wash. Put any scraps of left-over soap in the squeezy bottle, add some warm water and leave by the sink to wash your hands after cooking. It lasts for ages! When the suds get thin, put in more soap chips. If it gets too thick, just add more warm water.

6. Crushed cornflakes make a good crumble topping. Put the cornflakes in a bag and crush with a rolling pin. Mix with spices and honey and spoon over cooked fruit – no extra cooking necessary.

7. Kidney fat is cheaper than commercially prepared suet. Grate and store in a screw-top jar. It will keep in a refrigerator for a month.

8. When stewing rhubarb and plums, add $\frac{1}{2}$ teaspoon bicarbonate of soda to each pound of fruit – much less sugar will be needed. Bring the fruit and water to the boil, sprinkle on the bicarbonate, simmer for a minute and sweeten to taste.

9. To prevent bacon rashers shrinking and to make them go further, stretch them by rubbing the flat side of a kitchen knife along the slices.

EATING SENSIBLY

This is not a book on nutrition, but there are some things that are worth knowing. A good everyday diet must provide you with sufficient 'building' foods (protein, iron and calcium, and vitamins A, C and D), energy food (calories), B vitamins and cereal roughage. Meals are properly balanced when they give you enough of these foods. So a meal of braised beef with carrots and mashed potato, followed by pineapple, can be balanced by adding grilled tomatoes or sprouts for vitamin C and custard with the pineapple for calcium.

The table on page 28 has been devised to give you some information about the value of the foods you eat. It shows which foods to choose for proteins, calories, vitamin C, etc. Some foods provide more than one value, for example, milk, cheese and 'fat' fish like herrings, kippers, sardines, etc., provide protein, calories and vitamins A and D.

Bread provides protein, calories, calcium, iron and B vitamins. Liver – all kinds – provides protein, iron, calories and B vitamins. Tomatoes provide vitamins A and C – and roughage. But sugar provides calories *only*.

Try to eat some of these foods every day – milk, cheese, bread, margarine, bacon (or oatmeal if you are vegetarian); choose a food which is a good source of iron, and an orange or another fruit rich in vitamin C.

FOOD VALUES

FOODS FOR BUILDING AND REPAIR

Protein foods

All kinds of:

Milk
Cheese
Meat
Fish
Bread
Flour
Nuts
Pork and Bacon
Black pudding
Tripe
Liver
Kidney
Heart
Poultry
Eggs
Oily fish
Shell fish
Dried peas
Dried beans
Lentils
Baked beans
Cereals
Rice
Oats and
    oatmeal

Iron-rich foods

Curry (richest)
Cocoa
Liver
Kidney
Heart
Faggots
Black pudding
Beef
Corned beef
Sardines
Brisling
Dried figs
Dried apricots
Prunes
Oatmeal
Almonds
Lentils
Breads
Shell fish
Plain chocolate

Vitamins A and D

Whole milk (A)
Cheese (A)
Butter (A)
Liver (A)
Eggs (A and D)
Margarine
    (A and D)
Oily fish
    (A and D)
Tomatoes (A)
Dried apricots
    (A)
Prunes (A)
Red peppers (A)
Cream, double
    (A)
Broccoli (A)
Carrots, fresh and
    canned (A)

Vitamin C

Fruits/Vegetables,
    fresh, frozen
    and canned
All citrus fruits
    and juices
Blackcurrants
Strawberries
Gooseberries
Tomatoes
Broccoli
Cabbage
Swedes
Cauliflower
Sprouts
Red peppers
Green peppers
New potatoes

Calcium foods

All kinds of:

Milk
Cheese
White bread
White flour
Tripe
Sardines
Pilchards
Figs
Almonds
Treacle
Salmon

FOODS FOR MUSCULAR ENERGY

Calorie-rich

Butter
Margarine
Lard
Oils
Cream, double
Cheese
Fat fish
Sardines
Tuna
Salmon
Fat meat
Fat bacon
Oats
Oatmeal
Bread
Flour
Bran cereals
Rice
Pasta
Semolina
Cornflour
Pearl barley
Potatoes, new
Potatoes, old
Potato crisps
Potato chips
Sugar
Jam
Syrup
Treacle
Sweets
Cakes and mixes
Biscuits
Nuts
Plain chocolate

Vitamins B

Lean pork and
    bacon
Bacon and pork
    products
Ham loaf
Salami
Luncheon meat
Liver
Heart
Kidney
Liver paste
Bread
Flour
Dried yeast
Yeast extract
Dried peas
Dried beans
Lentils
Peanuts,
    unsalted
Brazil nuts
Almonds

Cereal roughage

Brown flour
Brown bread
Oats and
    oatmeal
All Bran
Bran Buds
Swiss-style
    cereal
Digestive biscuits
Crispbreads

Note: Foods printed in **bold** type have more than one food value

THE CALORIE COUNTER

Food provides the fuel for our bodies, producing the energy to keep us alive, warm and moving around, and this fuel is measured in calories. We need to eat enough of the 'fuel foods' to *balance* the calories of muscular energy we spend each day. The main point to remember is that, if you eat more calories than your body needs, over a period of time you'll put on weight. An average woman under fifty-five spends and needs about 2200 calories of energy daily and a man 2700. (After the age of fifty-five a woman only needs 1800 calories and a man 2300.) So to maintain a constant weight one must eat foods which will supply this amount of calories. If you eat an extra 500 calories every day, then this surplus 'fuel food' will be stored in your body as *fat* – and your weight is likely to increase at the rate of 1 lb per week! Eating those extra unnecessary calories is very easy and painless: *another* slice of cake, sugar in your tea, a larger helping of spaghetti – *so be warned*!

To simplify calorie counting, the chart below divides food into straightforward *100-calorie portions*.

Bread, buns and breadcrumbs
1 large slice of any type of bread
1 roll
½ bun or teacake
1 small scone
1 crumpet
2 slices crispbread
3 heaped tablespoons fresh breadcrumbs

Cakes and biscuits
1 small wedge of any type of cake
1 rock cake
1 shortbread 'finger'
1 sweet or cream-filled biscuit
3 semi-sweet biscuits, e.g., digestive

2 cream crackers, water biscuits or any cheese biscuit
½ a normal size pastry (a rich one)

Chocolates and sweets
4 small squares of any sort of chocolate
2 individual chocolates
4 toffees, bullseyes, acid drops or any other sweets

Butter, cooking fats and oils
1 large walnut-sized piece (½ oz) of any type of butter or
   margarine
1 level tablespoon *peanut* butter
1 tablespoon of any kind of oil
1 small walnut-sized piece of any of the solid fats: lard, suet,
   dripping

Cereals
1 breakfastcup Cornflakes, Sugar Puffs, Rice Crispies, etc.
¾ teacup All-Bran, Bran Buds
2 rounded tablespoons wheatgerm
1 heaped tablespoon oatmeal
2 heaped tablespoons rolled oats

Cheese
1 thin slice, 2 × 3 inches, or 1 oz of any of the full-fat cheeses,
   e.g., Derby, Cheddar, Cheshire, Lancashire, Stilton,
   Blue cheese
1 slightly thicker slice or 1½ oz of any of the low-fat cheeses,
   e.g., Edam, Camembert
¾ small carton of curd cheese
1 small carton (4 oz) low-fat cottage cheese
1 rounded tablespoon cream cheese

Eggs
1 large or 2 small eggs, raw, boiled or poached

Fish
1 small (10-oz) whole white fish, e.g., whiting, plaice,

sole, etc. (the fish should be weighed with the bone but without its head)

A 5-oz white fish fillet, fresh or smoked, e.g., cod, haddock, etc.

2½ oz of any white fish in batter or breadcrumbs

1 small or ½ large whole herring, mackerel or kipper

1 large herring, mackerel or kipper fillet

2 oz rollmops

2 canned sardines

1½ oz any other canned fish, e.g., salmon, tuna, mackerel

2 fried 'Fish Fingers'

1 small teacup or a small (3-oz) can of shrimps, prawns, mussels, crab

Fruits, fresh, canned and dried, and fruit juices

2–3 medium-sized unpeeled apples

2–3 medium-sized unpeeled pears

2 medium-sized oranges

1 banana

2 grapefruit

7 oz (medium-sized bunch) of grapes

8 oz stoned fresh fruits, e.g. apricots, cherries, plums

1 small (5-oz) can stoned fruits with juice

8 oz fresh or frozen berry fruits

1 breakfast cup sweetened fruit juice

3–4 slices canned pineapple

⅓ pint fresh or canned orange juice

¼ medium-sized avocado

1 heaped tablespoon mixed dried fruit

2 dried figs

4–5 dried dates

½ teacup (2 oz) dried apricots

1 teacup (2½ oz) dried prunes (with stones)

Meats, poultry and sausages

2 oz *raw* fresh beef, pork or lamb

2½ oz *raw* liver, any kind

3½ oz kidney

6 oz tripe

½ of a 6-oz *grilled* pork or lamb chop (weighed with the bone)

2½ oz *raw* or *cooked* chicken, without bones, or 3½ oz with the bone, i.e., 1 leg

3 oz *raw or cooked* turkey, with the bone

1½ oz *cooked* meats, beef, pork, lamb, corned beef, ham loaf, tongue, luncheon meat

2 oz (2 slices) brawn

1 oz any kind of sausage (about ⅓ a sausage) or sausagemeat

1 thin rasher raw bacon (¾–1 oz)

1 oz *raw* gammon, ham

¾ oz *cooked* ham

Milk, cream and yogurt

¼ pint (5 fluid oz) fresh milk

4 tablespoons evaporated milk

1 heaped tablespoon low-fat milk powder

1 small carton (5 oz) of any kind of whole-fat yogurt

2 small cartons of any kind of low-fat yogurt

2 level tablespoons fresh single cream

1 level tablespoon fresh double cream

1 heaped tablespoon canned cream

Nuts – all highly calorific

1 rounded tablespoon (½ oz) salted peanuts

3 large shelled brazils

12 shelled almonds

4 shelled walnuts

1 level tablespoon (½ oz) ground almonds

Pastas and pulses

1 oz of any of the following – macaroni, noodles, spaghetti

1¼ oz dried *uncooked* peas, beans, lentils

1 small can baked beans in tomato sauce or butter beans

1 rounded tablespoon (1 oz) rice, pearl barley

Soups

1 small can thick undiluted soup

½ pint packet soup, when reconstituted
¾ pint of any thin soup.

Sugar
4 teaspoons, 7 large lumps or 1 oz of any kind of sugar

Vegetables and salads
Most green and root vegetables and salads have such insignificant calorie value that you can eat as much as you like, but remember that the knob of butter melting on top of hot vegetables or the generous dollop of salad cream will add calories:

2 level tablespoons salad cream or 1 level tablespoon of mayonnaise equals 100 calories

The main exception to the above is the *very* calorific spud, and each of the following is equal to 100 calories:

1 medium potato, baked, boiled or steamed
1 small teacup fresh mashed potato
1 rounded tablespoon instant mashed potato powder
6 chips
1 small packet crisps

Other vegetable portions which equal 100 calories quite quickly are:

1 medium-sized parsnip
1 medium-size (7 oz) beetroot
1 corn on the cob
1 teacup canned sweetcorn
1 teacup fresh or frozen peas (raw or cooked)

Wines, spirits and soft drinks
1 large wine glass dry wine, red or white
1 small wine glass sweet wine, red or white
1 small glass sherry
½ pint cider, dry or sweet
½ pint beer, pale ale, brown ale, etc.
3 tablespoons of any 70° proof spirits

½ pint Cola, fruit cordials, bitter lemon
Tonic water has practically no calories

Odds and ends
- 1 heaped tablespoon drinking chocolate, malted milk or cocoa
- 1 rounded tablespoon jam, syrup, treacle or honey
- 1 heaped tablespoon sweet chutneys
- 2 oz ice cream, any kind
- 1½ oz (⅓ packet) jelly
- 2 heaped tablespoons stuffing mix or *dried* breadcrumbs
- 2 level tablespoons packet sauce mixes (before making up)
- 1 heaped tablespoon of any kind of flour, cornflour or custard powder

---

A day's food can be easily counted in calories, using this method:

		Calories
Early morning tea	1 cup of tea with milk (no sugar)	25
Breakfast	¼ pint orange juice	50
	1 egg	100
	1 small lean rasher bacon	100
	1 large slice bread	100
	Few mushrooms (cooked in fat from bacon)	0
	Black coffee	0
Elevenses	1 cup Bovril	0
	1 cheese biscuit	50
Lunch	Lettuce/tomato salad	0
	1 large slice bread	100
	¼ oz butter	50
	2 oz cheese	200
	1 yogurt (low fat)	50
Tea	2 cups of tea with milk (but without sugar)	50
	1 semi-sweet biscuit	50

Supper	'Pork and Corn Parcel'	
	4 oz lean pork	200
	¼ oz butter or 3 tablespoons oil	100
	½ teacup sweetcorn	50
	Spices, mustard	0
	Cauliflower	0
	1 orange	50
Night cap	Hot chocolate made with ¼ pint milk	150
	DAY'S TOTAL	1475

As you have spare calories to spend you can still have some crisps, chocolate biscuits, a glass of beer, etc.

FOOD STORAGE

The information in this section has been reproduced with the kind permission of the Good Housekeeping Institute.

REFRIGERATOR STORAGE

The following notes should help you to use your refrigerator to best advantage, while the chart on pp. 37–39 is intended to give an indication of how long certain foods will keep under refrigeration.

1. All foods must be covered.

2. Allow hot dishes to cool before storing them, or the ice-making compartment will quickly become covered with frost, and this insulating layer will make it difficult for the air to be satisfactorily cooled.

3. Put in correct part of the refrigerator:

(a) Raw foods such as meat, bacon, poultry and fish should be kept directly under the frozen food compartment, in the coldest part of the refrigerator.

(b) Cooked meat and made-up dishes can go on the middle shelves.

(c) Vegetables, salad ingredients and bread go at the bottom, vegetables and salads in the crisper, if any.

(d) There is usually a compartment inside the door for butter, where it will not become too hard.

4. The 'edge' is taken off the flavour of many foods when they are chilled, so if possible remove such items as cheese, cold meats, salads, sandwiches, etc., from the refrigerator a little while before using them – the time depends on the room temperature. From the cooking angle, eggs and fats should be warmed up before baking time.

5. Wipe up any spilt foods at once, before they harden, and check the contents of the shelves regularly.

6. Defrost the refrigerator regularly, and clean it, using a weak solution of bicarbonate of soda in warm water.

Many refrigerator manufacturers are now labelling the freezer compartment of their refrigerator with a Star Rating, depending on the temperature of the Frozen Food Compartment (see table below).

Maximum temperature of frozen food compartment	Maximum storage time for (a) frozen foods, (b) ice cream	
*** 0°F	2–3 months	2–3 months
** + 10°F	4 weeks	1–2 weeks
* + 21°F	1 week	1 day

Refrigerator storage times

Food	How to store	Days
Meat, raw		
Joints, chops, cut meat	Rinse blood away; wipe dry, cover with polythene or foil	3–5 2–4
Minced meat, offal	Cover as above	1–2
Sausages	Cover as above	3
Bacon	Wrap in foil or polythene, or put in plastic container	7
Meat, cooked		
Joints, sliced ham	In tightly wrapped foil or polythene, or in lidded container	3–5 2–3
Continental sausages	In tightly wrapped foil or polythene, or in lidded container	3–5
Casseroles	In tightly wrapped foil or polythene, or in lidded container	2–3
Poultry, raw		
Whole or joints	Draw, wash, wipe dry. Wrap in polythene or foil	2–3
Poultry, cooked		
Whole or joints	Remove stuffing; when cool wrap or cover as for cooked meats	2–3
Made-up dishes	Cover when cool	1
Fish, raw (white, oily, smoked)	Cover loosely in foil or polythene	1–2
Fish, cooked	As for raw, or in covered container	2

Food	How to store	Days
Shellfish	Eat the day it is bought — don't store	

Vegetables, salads

Food	How to store	Days
Prepared green and root vegetables, green beans, celery, courgettes, aubergines, peppers	In crisper drawer, or in plastic container, or wrapped in polythene	5–8
Sweetcorn, mushrooms, tomatoes, radishes, spring onions	Clean or wipe as necessary; store in covered container	5–7
Lettuce, cucumber, cut onion, cut peppers, parsley	Clean or wipe as necessary; store in covered container	4–6
Cress, watercress	Clean or wipe as necessary; store in covered container	2

Fresh fruit

Food	How to store	Days
Cut oranges, grapefruit, lemons	In covered container	3–4
Strawberries, redcurrants, raspberries, peaches	In covered container	1–3
Grapes, cherries, gooseberries, cut melon	In covered container	5–7
Rhubarb, cleaned	In covered container	6–10

Eggs

Food	How to store	Days
Fresh, in shell	In rack, pointed end down	14
Yolks	In lidded plastic container	2–3
Whites	In lidded plastic container	3–4
Hard-boiled, in shell	Uncovered	up to 7

Food	How to store	Days
Fats		
Butter, margarine	In original wrapper, in special compartment of refrigerator	14–21
Cooking fats	In original wrapper, in special compartment of refrigerator	28
Milk, etc.		
Milk	In original container, closed	3–4
Cream	In original container, closed	2–4
Soured cream, butter-milk, yogurt	In original container, closed	7
Milk sweets, custards	Lightly covered with foil or film	2
Cheese		
Parmesan, in piece	In film, foil or airtight container	21–28

LARDER AND FOOD-CUPBOARD STORAGE

A larder, if cool and ventilated, gives the next best storage after a refrigerator – in fact, for some foods it's preferable – but many homes nowadays have only non-ventilated food-storage cupboards, which are of more limited usefulness.

The following notes are intended as helpful guidelines to larder and food-cupboard storage, while the chart on pp. 41–44 is intended as a handy reference to the keeping qualities of the different kinds of foodstuffs stored.

1. All food stored in a larder or cupboard should be kept in covered containers or suitable wrappings. Containers with closely fitting lids are recommended for non-perishable foods, especially those of a granular or powdery texture,

which clog in moist conditions. Airtight containers are essential for commodities whose flavour is vital, such as coffee and spices, and for crisp-textured biscuits, etc.

2. Foods for long-term larder storage should be placed on the higher or less accessible shelves, while perishables and regularly used foods should be close at hand. Use foods in the order in which they were bought, putting new purchases at the back of the shelves.

3. Food bought in packets, e.g., flour and sugar, may be stored in that way until opened; then the contents should be transferred to airtight containers. Labelling is important, especially when the foods look alike.

4. Quick-dried foods, such as peas, packet soups and some packaged foods, deteriorate when exposed to air, heat and moisture, but may be stored satisfactorily in the unopened packet or airtight jar if kept in a dry, cool place.

5. Canned foods should have the date of purchase marked on the label and should be used in rotation. Discard any 'blown' cans, shown by bulged ends and leaking seams. If, however, you see a cheap buy in a dented can, this is safe, provided that there is no sign of rust or seepage from the seams, but use up such cans quickly.

6. Most canned foods are perfectly sound for periods longer than given in the chart, but excessively long storage may mean that flavour and texture are not so good.

7. Don't store dog and cat cereals, biscuits, etc., in the larder – any infestation that might be present could spread rapidly to other commodities. (If this should happen, all affected food stuff must be destroyed and the container washed, sterilised and well dried before re-use.)

Larder and food-cupboard storage times

Times refer to unopened packets, jars or cans. Perishables

such as fish, meat, poultry, milk, cream, should be stored for
only about 1 day, covered as for refrigerator storage.

Food	Keeping qualities, time	Storage comments
Flour, white Wheatmeal Wholemeal	Up to 6 months Up to 3 months Up to 1 month	Once opened, transfer to container with close-fitting lid
Baking powder, bicarbonate of soda, cream of tartar	2–3 months	Dry storage essential; if opened, put in container with close-fitting lid
Dried yeast Cornflour, custard powder	Up to 6 months Good keeping qualities	As above As above
Pasta Rice, all types	As above As above	As above As above
Sugar, loaf, caster, granulated	As above	Cool, dry storage; if opened, transfer as above
Sugar, icing, brown	Limited life- tends to absorb moisture	Buy in small quantities, as required
Tea	Limited life – loses flavour if stored long	Buy in small quantities; store in airtight container in dry, cool place
Instant and ground coffee in sealed can or jar	Up to 1 year	Cool, dry storage; once opened, re-seal securely; use quickly

Food	Keeping qualities, time	Storage comments
Coffee beans, loose ground coffee	Very limited life; use immediately	Buy as required; use airtight container
Instant low-fat skimmed milk	3 months	Cool, dry storage is vital; once opened, re-seal securely; use fairly quickly
Breakfast cereals	Limited life	Buy in small quantities. Cool, dry place
Dehydrated foods	Up to 1 year	Cool, dry place. If opened, fold packet down tightly and use within a week
Herbs, spices, seasonings	6 months	Cool, dry storage, in airtight container. Keep from light. Buy in small quantities
Nuts, ground almonds, desiccated coconut	Limited life – depends on freshness when bought. Fat content goes rancid if kept too long	Lidded container
Dried fruits	2–3 months	Cool, dry storage
Jams, etc.	Good keeping quality	Dry, cool, dark storage
Honey, clear or thick	As above	Dry, cool storage. After about 1 year, appearance may alter, but honey is still fit to eat
Golden syrup, treacle	As above	As above

Food	Keeping qualities, time	Storage comments
Condensed milk	4–6 months	Safe even after some years, but caramelises and thickens. Once opened, harmless crust forms; cover can with foil lid and use within 1 month
Evaporated milk	6–8 months	Safe even after some years, but darkens, thickens and loses flavour. Once opened, treat as fresh milk
Canned fruit	12 months	Cool, dry place
Canned vegetables	2 years	Cool, dry place
Canned fish in oil	Up to 5 years	Cool, dry place
Canned fish in tomato sauce	Up to 1 year	Cool, dry place
Canned meat	Up to 5 years	As above. Cans holding 1 kilo or more should be kept in refrigerator
Canned ham	6 months	
Chutneys	Limited life	As above
Vinegars	Good keeping qualities – at least up to 2 years	Cool, dry, dark place; strong light affects flavoured vinegar and produces a non-bacterial cloudiness. Re-seal after use; never return unused vinegar to bottle

Food	Keeping qualities, time	Storage comments
Pickles, sauces	Reasonably good keeping qualities	Cool, dry, dark place
Oils (olive, corn)	Up to 18 months	Cool, dry place

HANDY MEASURES

Almonds, ground	1 oz = $3\frac{3}{4}$ level tsps	
Breadcrumbs, fresh	1 oz = 7	,, ,,
dried	1 oz = $3\frac{1}{4}$	,, ,,
Butter, lard, margarine	1 oz = 2	,, ,,
Cheese, Cheddar grated	1 oz = 3	,, ,,
Chocolate, grated	1 oz = $3\frac{1}{4}$	,, ,,
Cocoa	1 oz = $2\frac{3}{4}$	,, ,,
Coconut, dessicated	1 oz = 5	,, ,,
Coffee, instant	1 oz = $6\frac{1}{2}$	,, ,,
Coffee, ground	1 oz = 4	,, ,,
Cornflour, custard powder	1 oz = $2\frac{1}{2}$	,, ,,
Curry powder	1 oz = 5	,, ,,
Flour, unsifted	1 oz = 3	,, ,,
Ginger, ground	1 oz = $4\frac{1}{2}$	,, ,,
Rice, uncooked	1 oz = $1\frac{1}{2}$	,, ,,
Sugar, granulated or caster	1 oz = 2	,, ,,
icing	1 oz = $2\frac{1}{2}$	,, ,,
Syrup, unheated	1 oz = 1	,, ,,
Yeast, granulated	1 oz = $1\frac{1}{2}$	,, ,,

Liquid ingredients — water, milk, corn oil:

2 tablespoons	= $1\frac{1}{4}$ fl. oz	= $\frac{1}{16}$ pint
4 ,,	= $2\frac{1}{2}$ fl. oz	= $\frac{1}{8}$ pint
6 ,,	= $3\frac{3}{4}$ fl. oz	= $\frac{3}{16}$ pint
8 ,,	= 5 fl. oz	= $\frac{1}{4}$ pint

TEMPERATURES

OVEN TEMPERATURES

	Centigrade	Fahrenheit	Gas Mark
Very slow	135°C	275°F	1
Slow	149°C	300°F	2
Very moderate	163°C	325°F	3
Moderate	177°C	350°F	4
Moderately hot	190°C	375°F	5
Fairly hot	204°C	400°F	6
Hot	218°C	425°F	7
Very hot	232°C	450°F	8

FRYING TEMPERATURES

(Oil or fat for deep frying.)
If you have no thermometer, judge the heat by the time taken to brown a 1-inch cube of bread.

Doughnuts, fritters, onions, uncooked fish
350–360°F 60 seconds

Croquettes, cooked food
360–380°F 40 seconds

Potato chips, crisps, straws
370–390°F 20 seconds

METRIC CONVERSIONS

If you want to convert recipes from imperial to metric, we recommend that you use 25 grammes as a basic unit in place of 1 oz, 500 ml in place of 1 pint, and take the new British Standard 5-ml and 15-ml spoons in place of the old variable teaspoon and tablespoons; these adaptations will give a slightly smaller recipe quantity.

For more exact conversions and general reference, the following tables will be helpful:

DRY MEASURES
g=gramme; kg=kilogramme

1 oz	= 28.35 g	2 lb	= 907 g
4 oz ($\frac{1}{4}$ lb)	= 113 g	3 lb	= 1.36 kg
8 oz ($\frac{1}{2}$ lb)	= 227 g	4 lb	= 1.81 kg
16 oz (1 lb)	= 454 g	5 lb	= 2.27 kg
$1\frac{1}{2}$ lb	= 681 g	10 lb	= 4.54 kg

LIQUID MEASURES
ml=millilitre; l=litre

$\frac{1}{4}$ pint	= 142 ml	$1\frac{3}{4}$ pints	= 994 ml
$\frac{1}{2}$ pint	= 284 ml	2 pints	= 1.14 l
$\frac{3}{4}$ pint	= 426 ml	$2\frac{1}{2}$ pints	= 1.42 l
1 pint	= 568 ml	3 pints	= 1.70 l
$1\frac{1}{4}$ pints	= 710 ml	$3\frac{1}{2}$ pints	= 1.99 l
$1\frac{1}{2}$ pints	= 852 ml		

LENGTH
cm=centimetre

1 inch = 2.54 cm	1 foot = 30.48 cm

2   Soups, Stews and Casseroles

There is nothing more heartening on a cold day than a bowl of steaming soup or a tasty stew. These stews and casseroles are all simple to prepare and as they all reheat very well – and taste even better the second day – the recipes are for double quantities. So unless you're absolutely starving you're preparing two meals at once; this saves time, yours and the oven, and effort. Please read the notes on reheating foods as this is important, and remember that if you make a casserole on Monday and then want to eat the rest on Wednesday, you *must* boil it up thoroughly on the Tuesday.

Most of these dishes can be cooked on top or in the oven to suit you and your cooking equipment. It's very nice to have fancy cooking pots, but it's not really necessary – any stout pan or baking dish will do – and remember that kitchen foil makes a perfect lid. If you do think of investing in a new casserole, there are lots of practical and pretty ones around. Pyroflam and Le Creuset, for example, both make pans which can be used either on top or in the oven – they also guarantee even heat and easily cleaned surfaces and they last for ages.

SOUPS

Goulash Soup

6–8 oz stewing steak, cut into very small pieces
1 level tablespoon seasoned flour
1 large onion, sliced
1–2 tablespoons cooking oil
1 teaspoon paprika
1 dessertspoon tomato purée
1 pint beef stock (use water and 1 beef stock cube)
1 small can new potatoes
Salt and pepper

Shake the meat in seasoned flour in a paper bag. Fry the onions in the hot oil until golden brown, add the meat and brown well. Add the paprika, tomato purée and stock, and season to taste with salt and pepper. Simmer for 1 hour. Add the drained potatoes and allow to heat through.

Scotch Broth

1½ oz pearl barley
½ lb middle neck or breast of lamb
1 medium onion, chopped
1 carrot, diced
1 small turnip, diced
1 leek, sliced (optional)
Salt and pepper

Wash the pearl barley, cover with cold water and leave to soak for at least 4 hours. Put the meat in a casserole with 1 pint cold water. Add the vegetables and the drained pearl barley. Season with salt and pepper and simmer on the stove or in the oven at 325°F/Gas Mark 3 for 2 hours. Remove from the oven and leave to cool. Skim off any surface fat, before reheating.

Notes
If preferred, rice can be used instead of barley. There is no need to soak the rice beforehand – add it to the soup with the vegetables.

If you have any fresh parsley, chop 1–2 tablespoons and sprinkle on top before serving.

Chicken Giblet Soup

½–¾ lb chicken giblets – heart, liver, gizzard, neck
2 carrots, chopped
1 onion, chopped
1½ pints water
1 chicken stock cube
Salt and pepper

½ oz dripping, butter or margarine
1 tablespoon flour

Put the giblets in a pan, cover with the cold water and bring slowly to the boil. Skim off any scum from the surface. Add the vegetables, water and crumbled stock cube. Add salt and pepper and simmer gently for 1½ hours until the giblets are tender. Pour the soup through a sieve or strainer, into a bowl. Cut the giblets, except the neck, which is left whole, into small pieces and put aside. Melt the dripping, butter or margarine in the pan, stir in the flour and gradually add the soup. Stir until boiling, add the giblet pieces and simmer for a few minutes before serving.

Kidney Soup

½ oz butter
2 teaspoons cooking oil
½ onion, chopped
2 lamb's kidneys
2 oz mushrooms, chopped
1 oz flour
1 pint stock (use water and a stock cube)
1 bay leaf
Pinch of thyme
Salt
Black pepper
1 tablespoon sherry (optional)

Heat the butter and oil in a saucepan and fry the chopped onion until soft. Skin the kidneys, remove the cores and dice in ½-inch cubes. Add the kidneys to the pan, fry for a few minutes over a low heat and then add the mushrooms. Stir in the flour and stock, and add the herbs, salt and black pepper. Simmer for 30 minutes and add the sherry.

Note
Serve with fried bread – try cooking the bread in butter or margarine flavoured with some of the kidney fat.

Fisherman's Soup

4–5 slices of bread, $\frac{1}{2}$ inch thick
$1\frac{1}{2}$ oz butter
3 oz grated cheese
1 large onion, thinly sliced
Tomato purée
Water

Toast the slices of bread and, when cold, butter thickly.
Put a layer of buttered toast in an ovenproof dish or basin
and top with a good layer of grated cheese, a layer of thinly
sliced onion lightly browned in butter and a thin layer of
tomato purée. Repeat the layers until the basin is two-thirds
full. Finish with a layer of grated cheese. Pour boiling water
gently in at the side until just visible. Bake uncovered in a
low oven for $1\frac{1}{2}$ hours, adding more water if necessary until
there is a delicious purée with a crisp and golden top crust.
Marvellous on a cold day.

Corn Chowder

2 rashers streaky bacon, trimmed and diced
$\frac{1}{2}$ small onion, chopped
1 stick celery, sliced
$\frac{1}{2}$ pint water
1 medium potato, diced (fresh or canned)
Pinch of paprika
$\frac{1}{2}$ bay leaf
Salt
$1\frac{1}{2}$ tablespoons flour
$\frac{1}{2}$ pint milk
1 small can sweetcorn

Fry the bacon, onion and celery together for a few minutes.
Pour on the water and add the potato, paprika and bay
leaf. Season with salt. Bring to the boil and simmer for
10–15 minutes. Blend the flour and 2 tablespoons of the milk

together. Add to the soup and bring to the boil again, stirring all the time. Gradually stir in the remaining milk and sweetcorn and taste for seasoning.

Fast French Onion Soup

1 large onion
½ oz margarine or 1 tablespoon cooking oil
½ pint stock (use water and 1 beef or chicken stock cube)
1 teaspoon Worcester sauce
Salt and pepper
1 slice bread
1 oz grated cheese

Peel the onion and slice thinly. Heat the margarine or oil in a pan and cook the onion over a gentle heat until golden — about 5 minutes. Pour the stock over the onion and add the Worcester sauce. Season with salt and pepper. Simmer gently for 10 minutes. Pour into a fireproof bowl, top with a slice of toast and sprinkle on the grated cheese. Place under a hot grill for a minute to melt the cheese.

Spinach Soup

1 small packet frozen chopped spinach
½ oz butter
½ small onion, chopped
1 rounded tablespoon flour
½ pint chicken stock (use water and a stock cube)
¼ pint milk
Salt and pepper
Pinch of nutmeg (optional)
1 hard-boiled egg, finely chopped

Cook the spinach as directed on the packet and drain well. Melt the butter in a pan and cook the chopped onion until soft. Stir in the flour and stock, blend well and bring to the boil. Add the spinach, simmer for 15 minutes, add the milk and season to taste with salt and pepper. A pinch of nutmeg can be added. Add the finely chopped hard-boiled egg to the soup before serving.

Potato Soup

1 large potato per person
½ onion, sliced
Stock or water
Milk
Salt and pepper

For each bowl of soup, peel and dice 1 large potato. Put it in a pan with a slice of onion and cover with boiling water or stock. Season lightly with salt, cover and cook until the potato is very soft. Crush the potato with a fork, without draining. Add hot milk to make the soup as thin as you like it. Season with pepper.

Note
You can add some diced cheese, cooked vegetables or crumbled grilled bacon to the soup before serving.

STEWS AND CASSEROLES

Pork Fillet with Prunes and Cider

1 small pork fillet, 8–10 oz
6 prunes
1 cup left-over tea
1 bacon rasher
Pinch of sage
Salt and pepper
4–5 tablespoons cider

Gently simmer the prunes in the tea until plump and tender. Remove the stones. Cut three-quarters of the way through the fillet lengthwise. Stuff the cavity with the prunes, sprinkle on the sage and season with salt and pepper. Press the fillet firmly together to retain its shape. Remove the bacon rind and cut the rasher into ¼-inch strips. Wrap these strips round the fillet and place the meat in a greased baking dish. Pour the cider over and roast at 375°F/Gas Mark 5 for 30 minutes, or until cooked through, basting frequently with the pan juices. Serve hot with the pan juices and new potatoes.

Eat the rest of the fillet cold the next day with salad.

Pork Special

1 pork leg steak or ½ lb lean pork
½ oz margarine
1 small onion, sliced
1 rounded tablespoon flour
1 small can tomatoes
2 oz mushrooms, sliced
Salt and pepper

Cut the pork into cubes. Heat the margarine in a pan and fry the pork cubes until golden. Remove from the pan to a small casserole. Fry the onion in the remaining fat until soft. Stir in the flour, cook for a couple of minutes and add the tomatoes and mushrooms. Season with salt and pepper. Bring to the boil, pour over the pork, cover and cook at 350°F/Gas Mark 4 for 1–1½ hours until tender. This dish can also be simmered very gently on top of the oven.

Pork, Potato and Tomato Casserole

1 lb fresh streaky pork
1 bay leaf
3–4 peppercorns
1 small onion, sliced

1 small can tomatoes
2–3 medium-sized potatoes, thickly sliced

Cut the pork into $\frac{1}{2}$-inch cubes and place in a pan with the tomatoes, onion and seasonings. Arrange the sliced potatoes on top, cover tightly and simmer on top of the oven for 1 hour.

Piquant Pork

2 tablespoons cooking oil or fat
1 onion, chopped
1 small clove garlic, crushed (optional)
$\frac{3}{4}$ lb lean pork, cut in small cubes
2–3 tablespoons tomato ketchup
$\frac{1}{2}$ teaspoon chilli powder
1 small can tomatoes
Salt and pepper

Heat the oil or fat and fry the onion and garlic until the onion is soft. Add the pork and cook for 5 minutes. Turn into a small casserole and add the remaining ingredients. Season with salt and pepper. Cover and cook for 45 minutes at 300°F/Gas Mark 2.

Lamb Casserole with Apple and Raisins

2–3 medium-sized potatoes, peeled and thinly sliced
1 small onion, sliced
1 cooking apple, peeled, cored and sliced
$\frac{3}{4}$ lb–1 lb stewing lamb
1 tablespoon raisins
$\frac{1}{4}$ teaspoon dried mixed herbs
2 teaspoons meat extract
$\frac{1}{4}$ pint hot water
Knob of butter or margarine
Salt and pepper

Put half the potato, onion and apple at the bottom of an

55

ovenproof dish or casserole. Put the lamb on top, add the raisins and herbs, and season with salt and pepper. Cover with the remaining apple and onion slices and finish with the remaining potato slices. Dissolve the meat extract in hot water and pour into the casserole. Dot the potatoes with small pieces of margarine. Cover and cook at 350°F/Gas Mark 4 for 1–1½ hours. Uncover and cook for a further 15–20 minutes until the potatoes are golden brown.

Lamb Hot-Pot

¾–1 lb stewing lamb
1 tablespoon flour
Cooking fat or oil
1 small onion, sliced
1 frozen stew pack of mixed vegetables or ½ lb fresh vegetables (carrots, potatoes, turnips) cut up very small
2 teaspoons tomato purée
2 tablespoons water
2–3 cooked potatoes (fresh or canned), sliced

Toss the lamb pieces in seasoned flour in a bag. Heat a little cooking fat or oil in a pan and cook the onion until golden brown. Add the meat and brown quickly on all sides. Add the contents of the stew pack, the tomato purée and water. Stir well together. Cover and simmer very gently on top of the stove or in the oven at 325°F/Mark 3 for 1½ hours.

When cooked, skim off any excess fat with a spoon and cover the top with the sliced potatoes. Spoon a little fat over the potatoes and brown under a medium grill.

Variations
½ hour before serving, add a small can of baked beans in tomato sauce or a can of processed peas, drained.

Curried Lamb with Apricots

¾–1 lb fillet, top leg or shoulder of lamb
1 tablespoon cooking oil
1 small onion, chopped
1 level teaspoon curry powder
1 level tablespoon flour
½ pint chicken stock (or water and a stock cube)
2 oz dried apricots, washed and chopped
2 teaspoons sultanas or raisins
2 level teaspoons sweet chutney

Cut the lamb into 2-inch pieces, removing as much fat as possible. Heat the oil in a frying pan, add the meat and brown all over. Remove from the pan. Add the chopped onion to the pan and cook gently for 5 minutes. Stir in the curry powder. Add the flour and cook for a couple of minutes. Pour on the stock and bring to the boil, stirring. Simmer for 5 minutes, uncovered, then add the apricots, chutney, sultanas and meat. Cover and simmer gently for 1–1½ hours on the stove or in the oven at 350°F/Gas Mark 4. Serve with boiled rice.

Casseroled Beef with Dumplings

½–1 lb stewing steak
1 tablespoon seasoned flour
1 onion, sliced
2 tablespoons cooking fat or oil
2 carrots, sliced
1 turnip, diced
2 potatoes, diced
1 bay leaf
Salt and pepper
¼ pint beef stock or water

Dumplings
2 oz self-raising flour (or plain flour and 1 level teaspoon baking powder)

57

1 oz shredded suet or fat
Pinch of salt

Cut the meat into cubes and toss in seasoned flour in a bag. Heat the fat or oil in a thick saucepan or casserole and brown the onions, then add the meat and brown on all sides. Add the other vegetables and the bay leaf and season with salt and pepper. Pour on the stock or water, bring to the boil, cover tightly and simmer gently for $1\frac{1}{2}$–2 hours at $325°$F/ Gas Mark 3 or on top of the oven until the meat is tender.

To make the dumplings: Add a generous pinch of salt to the flour and rub in the fat until the mixture resembles breadcrumbs. Mix to a firm light dough with cold water. Form into balls – not too large as the dumplings will swell to twice their size. Add to the stew 20–30 minutes before serving.

Notes

For a change, add a pinch of mustard powder or $\frac{1}{4}$ teaspoon dried mixed herbs to the dumpling mixture.

Dumplings can also be cooked in soup or in a pan of boiling water. Put the lid on the pan and boil for 15–20 minutes.

The Easiest Beef Stew

$\frac{1}{2}$–$\frac{3}{4}$ lb stewing steak
1 tablespoon seasoned flour
1 onion, sliced
3 carrots, sliced
$\frac{1}{4}$ pint beef stock or water
1 bay leaf
2–3 potatoes, fresh or canned, thinly sliced
Salt and pepper

Cut the meat into cubes. Toss the meat, sliced carrots and onion in seasoned flour in a bag. Place in a casserole. Pour over the stock or water and add the bay leaf. Season with salt and pepper. Cover tightly and cook over a low heat or in the oven at 300°F/Gas Mark 1 for 1½–2 hours, or until the meat is tender. Twenty minutes before serving, place the sliced potatoes on top – this absorbs any fat.

Braised Beef in Beer

½–¾ lb stewing steak
1 tablespoon seasoned flour
½ oz margarine or cooking oil
1 onion, sliced
2 teaspoons brown sugar
¼ pint pale or brown ale

Cut the meat into cubes and toss in flour in a bag. Heat the margarine or oil and fry the meat until lightly browned on all sides. Remove the meat and fry the onion slices for 2–3 minutes. Place the meat and onion in a small ovenproof dish or casserole. Add the sugar and pour the beer over. Cover the dish tightly and cook at 325°F/Gas Mark 3 for 1½ hours until the meat is tender. This stew can also be cooked on top of the oven – allow to simmer gently. The gravy can be thickened with cornflour.

Notes

Just before serving, spread a little mustard on a few thin slices of bread and place these on top of the beef, sprinkle with grated cheese and brown under a low grill.

You could add the onion skin when you put in the beer – it gives extra colour and flavour.

Cobbler Topping

A tasty cobbler topping can be made: sift 2 oz self-raising flour with a pinch of salt. Rub in 1 oz shredded beef suet (or 1 oz mixed margarine and lard). Bind with 1½ tablespoons water. Roll out ½ inch thick and cut into small rounds. Raise the oven temperature to 425°F/Gas Mark 7. Put the topping on the casserole and bake uncovered for 15 minutes.

Susan's Stew

½–¾ lb stewing steak
6–8 small pickling onions or 1 large onion
4 small carrots, sliced
2 turnips, chopped
Juice of 1 small orange
½ pint stock or water
3–4 potatoes, peeled and chopped

Put all the ingredients into a pan, cover and cook in a low oven, 325°F/Gas Mark 3, for 1½–2 hours or simmer very gently on top of the stove.

Liver, Bacon and Onion Casserole

4 oz pig's liver
1 tablespoon seasoned flour
3 rashers streaky bacon
1 onion, sliced
Salt and pepper
6 tablespoons beef stock (use water and ¼ beef stock cube)

Slice the liver and toss in the seasoned flour. Trim the bacon rashers, cut into strips and place half at the bottom of a fireproof dish. Put half the onion slices on top, followed by the liver, the rest of the onion and finally the remaining bacon pieces. Season well between layers with salt and pepper. Add the stock, cover and cook at 350°F/Gas Mark 4 for 1 hour.

Notes

Pig's liver is a very good buy. If you sometimes find the flavour too strong, soak the liver in a little milk for several hours before using.

Extra uncooked liver should be covered, kept in a refrigerator and used the next day. Try cutting the liver into small, thin slices or matchsticks and tossing it in a little hot fat or oil. When the liver is almost cooked, add a tomato, cut in quarters, and cook for another few minutes.

Rabbit Casserole

1–2 rabbit joints
1 tablespoon seasoned flour
1 oz margarine or butter
1 small onion, chopped
2 oz rice
2 oz lentils
2 tomatoes, quartered
½ bay leaf
¼ pint stock or water

With a sharp knife, cut the rabbit meat off the bones in small pieces. Shake the pieces in seasoned flour and fry in the hot margarine or butter until golden brown. Add the onion, rice and lentils and continue frying until the rice is transparent. Add the tomatoes and bay leaf and season with salt and pepper. Pour on the stock or water. Stir well, bring to the boil, cover tightly and simmer until all the liquid is absorbed and the rice dry and separate, 20–30 minutes.

Notes
½ lb of streaky pork, cut in cubes, could be added to the casserole.

Oxtail in Ale

½ small oxtail (1 lb) cut in pieces
2 tablespoons cooking oil
1 medium onion, chopped
2 carrots, sliced
1 stick celery, sliced
1 bottle (9⅔ fl oz) light ale
1 bay leaf
Nutmeg (optional)
Salt and pepper

Trim any excess fat from the oxtail joints. Heat the oil in a frying pan and fry the joints until lightly browned on all sides. Drain and place in a casserole. Lightly brown the vegetables in the fat left in the frying pan and add to the casserole. Pour on the beer. Add the bay leaf, a grating of whole nutmeg and season with salt and pepper. Cover the casserole and cook at 325°F/Gas Mark 3 for 1½ hours; then lower the temperature to 300°F/Gas Mark 2 and continue cooking for 1½ hours. Remove the casserole from the oven and leave in a cool place overnight. Next day remove any surface fat, reheat and serve.

Notes

Oxtail is usually sold jointed, so it is quite simple to check that it contains sufficient meat. The meat should be bright red, with a moderate layer of firm white fat.

You could substitute 2 tablespoons vinegar for the ale – the acid will disappear completely in the cooking.

Kidney Casserole

2 lamb's kidneys
½ oz margarine
1 small onion, thinly sliced (or ½ large onion)
Flour
2 oz rice
1 (8–oz) can tomatoes
6 tablespoons stock (use water and ¼ stock cube)
Salt and pepper

Remove the fat and skin from the kidneys and cut out the hard core. Heat the margarine in a pan and cook the onion until soft. Slice the kidneys, roll in flour, add to the hot fat and brown quickly. Stir in the rice, the tomatoes with the juice and the stock. Season to taste with salt and pepper. Cover and simmer gently for 25 minutes, or until all the liquid has been absorbed.

Stuffed Heart

1 lamb's heart
2 tablespoons packet stuffing – parsley and thyme or sage and
  onion
Flour
½ oz dripping
2 carrots, sliced
1 small onion, sliced
1 stick of celery, sliced (optional)
1 tablespoon tomato sauce
¼ pint stock (use water and ½ stock cube)

Wash the heart well in cold water and trim away any fat, tubes or gristle with kitchen scissors or a sharp knife. Cut through the wall which divides the centre of the heart. Leave to soak in cold, salted water for ½–1 hour. Rinse and drain. Make up the stuffing as directed on the packet. Press this stuffing into the heart cavity and tie with string to make parcel. Coat the heart in flour. Heat the dripping in a pan and brown on all sides. Put the vegetables into a small casserole, place the heart on top, add the tomato sauce and cover with stock. Cook at 350°F/Gas Mark 4 for 1½ hours, turning the heart occasionally in the stock.

Notes
Chopped ham or bacon, parsley and grated lemon rind can be added to the stuffing.

Both lamb's and pig's hearts are suitable for stuffing and roasting.

One heart per portion is usually sufficient.

3 A Chapter on Chops – Lamb, Pork, Bacon

3

Chops have long been the mainstay of the single person and the cook who is in a hurry. It is probably because of this that the chop has acquired its reputation for being rather lowly and dull. Well, there's a host of recipes in this chapter which will help to dispel any thoughts like these. Grilled chops, stuffed chops, baked chops or chops wrapped in pastry – take your pick.

LAMB CHOPS

DIFFERENT SORTS

Best end of neck: Five or six pairs of ribs cut from next to the loin: should be chined or the back split so that it's easy to carve into chops. Known as cutlets when cut before cooking. (There is also a recipe for roasting a small best end of neck on p. 115.)

Chump chops: Leg end of loin. Compact and meaty with a small bone.

Loin chops: From the rib end of loin, with or without kidney; the T-shaped bone gives more bone-to-meat ratio. Should be more tender than chump. Buy these chops about 1 inch thick if possible. Best grilled or fried.

COOKING METHODS

Grilled

Plain

Place the chops on an oiled or greased rack 2 inches from the preheated grill. Grill for 1 minute on either side first, then about 5 minutes either side. Season with salt and pepper. Lamb chops may be grilled with the fat of one overlapping the lean of the next. The melting fat will baste the lean, keeping the chops moist and succulent.

With Herbs

Before grilling, sprinkle each chop with lemon juice and rosemary or oregano.

London Chops

Two minutes before the end of grilling mix 1 tablespoon marmalade with 1 teaspoon lemon juice, brush over the chop and continue grilling.

With Mint

Brush the chop with mint jelly a few minutes before the end of grilling time – the jelly melts and gives the meat a delicious flavour.

Cheesey Chop

Dip the chop in a little lightly beaten egg. Mix 2 tablespoons breadcrumbs with 1 tablespoon grated cheese. Coat the chops with this mixture. Grill at a high heat.

Chop on Toast

Toast one side of a thick slice of bread. Lightly butter the untoasted side. Place a chop on top, cut round the bread to fit, season with pepper, dot with butter and grill the chop on both sides.

Lemon and Ginger Chops

Marinade
2 tablespoons cooking oil
1 tablespoon lemon juice
2 teaspoons brown sugar
½ teaspoon ground ginger
Salt and pepper
1–2 chops

Mix all the marinade ingredients together. Place the chops in a shallow dish and pour the marinade over them. Leave for 2–3 hours, turning occasionally. Remove the chops and grill, turning the chops occasionally and basting them with the marinade.

Baked

Plain

Season the lamb chop with salt and pepper. Fry in a little hot fat until just brown. Place in a baking dish, pour on pan juices and bake at 350°F/Gas Mark 4 for 30 minutes, turning halfway through. The chops cook through without becoming burnt or dry.

In Foil

Cut a small garlic clove into thin slivers. With a sharp knife, spike the chops and insert the garlic slivers into the cuts. Sprinkle the chop with a little dried rosemary, wrap in foil and cook at 350°F/Gas Mark 4 for 30 minutes, pouring off the fat after 20 minutes.

Onion and Potato Bake

2 large potatoes, sliced
1 small onion, chopped
1 lamb chop
4–6 tablespoons stock (use water and ¼ stock cube)
Butter

Butter a small ovenproof dish and cover the bottom with a layer of the uncooked sliced potatoes. Add the chopped onion. Brown the chops in a little butter and add to the pan with any buttery juices. Add the stock, cover and bake at 350°F/Gas Mark 4 for 1 hour.

Saucy Lamb Chops

1–2 chops
1 tablespoon honey
1 tablespoon cooking oil
1 teaspoon lemon juice
½ teaspoon mixed herbs

Place the chops in an ovenproof dish. Put the honey, oil, lemon juice and mixed herbs in a pan and stir over a low heat until the honey has dissolved. Pour over the chops and leave in a cool place for 30 minutes. Bake in a pre-heated oven 350°F/Gas Mark 4 for 30–40 minutes until the chops are tender. Serve with rice and peas.

Lamb with Leeks

2 middle neck chops
2 leeks (halved)
1 can tomatoes
½ teaspoon paprika

Put all the ingredients in a casserole. Cover with a tight-fitting lid or foil. Cook at 350°F/Gas Mark 4 for 30–40 minutes, or until the chops are tender.

Lamb Chop in Pastry

2 oz self-raising flour
Pinch of salt
½ oz shredded suet or grated kidney fat
2 teaspoons chopped fresh mint or ½ teaspoon Colmans
  fresh garden mint (optional)
1 lamb chop

Sift the flour and salt into a bowl. Stir in the suet and chopped mint and mix with cold water to make a firm dough. Roll out thinly on a lightly floured surface. Place the chop in the centre and wrap the pastry around. Dampen the edges of the pastry to secure firmly. Turn the chop over and place in an ovenproof dish. Brush with a little milk or beaten egg and cook at 350°F/Gas Mark 4 for 45 minutes.

Fried

When frying lamb chops, use hot, shallow fat. Turn the chops quickly to seal in the juices, then reduce the heat and cook gently for 20–25 minutes.

Sweet and Sour Lamb

1–2 chops
1 tablespoon cooking oil
1½ level tablespoons cornflour
1 (7-oz) can pineapple pieces
1 chicken stock cube
3 tablespoons vinegar
1 tablespoon soy sauce
1 level teaspoon caster sugar

Fry the chops in the oil until cooked and golden brown. Remove from pan. Add the cornflour to the pan juices and stir until well blended. Make the drained pineapple syrup up to ¼ pint with water and add to the pan. Crumble in the stock cube and bring slowly to the boil, stirring. When the sauce has thickened, add the vinegar, soy sauce, sugar and pineapple pieces and return the chops to the pan. Simmer slowly, with a lid over the frying pan, for about 10 minutes.

PORK CHOPS

DIFFERENT SORTS

Chump chops: Compact and meaty, from the tail end. Good for frying, grilling, roasting.

Loin chops: Choicest cuts are from the hind loin; they have the eye of the meat, sometimes with the kidney. Although the flesh is delicate, there is a lot of bone. Chops from the foreloin, which have lean and fat interspersed, are more economical. Cutlets from the neck end loin have the sweet meat in a 'nut' surrounded by fat.

Spare rib chops: Fairly lean and meaty. Suitable for baking, braising and stewing.

COOKING METHODS

Grilled

Preheat the grill until red hot. Place the pork chop on a lightly greased grill rack. Grill the chop for 5 minutes on either side, reduce the heat to moderate and grill for a further 5–7 minutes according to thickness and cut.

Toppings

For a delicious topping, mix together equal quantities of brown sugar, dry mustard and melted butter or soft margarine. Spoon the mixture over the chop during the last 5 minutes under the grill.

Or try a spicy honey and mustard topping – mix 1 teaspoon dry mustard with 1 tablespoon honey and 1 teaspoon Worcester sauce. Grill the chops on one side, turn over and spread honey mixture on top. Continue grilling, basting occasionally.

Baked

Plain

Brush a pork chop with cooking oil, season with salt and pepper and sprinkle on a pinch of sage or marjoram. Cook, covered, for 35 minutes at 350°F/Gas Mark 4, then uncover and cook for a further 15 minutes.

Savoury Bake

1 pork chop
1 slice lemon
1 slice onion
1 level teaspoon brown sugar
1 teaspoon tomato ketchup

Top the chop with the lemon, onion, soft brown sugar and the ketchup. Cover the dish or casserole and bake in the oven at 350°F/Gas Mark 4 for 30 minutes, then uncover and cook for a further 20–30 minutes, basting occasionally.

Spicy Bake

Marinade
1 tablespoon soy sauce
1 tablespoon lemon juice
2 teaspoons brown sugar
A little sliced onion

1 pork chop
Cooking fat

Mix the first four ingredients and pour over the chop. Leave to marinade for an hour. Remove the chop and brown in hot fat. Pour over the marinade, cover and bake at 350°F/Gas Mark 4 for 45 minutes.

Pork, Mushroom and Pepper

1 small onion, chopped
½ green pepper, thinly sliced
2 oz mushrooms, sliced
Stock
1 tablespoon tomato purée
1 teaspoon lemon juice
Pinch of sugar
1 pork chop
Cooking fat

Fry the chop until brown on both sides. Turn into a casserole and add the chopped onion, the thinly sliced green pepper and the sliced mushrooms. Dissolve ½ beef stock cube in 4 tablespoons hot water and add the tomato purée, a pinch of sugar and the lemon juice. Mix well, pour over the meat, cover and cook at 350°F/Gas Mark 4 for 45 minutes.

Sage and Onion Chop

Put the chop on an ovenproof dish and spread a layer of sage and onion stuffing mix over the lean part. Cover with a greased paper and bake at 350°F/Gas Mark 4 until the lean part is well cooked and the fat crisp and brown – 45 minutes approx.

Fruity Pork

Seasoned flour
½ small onion, chopped
1 small can apricot halves
2 teaspoons soy sauce
1 pork chop
Cooking oil

Shake the chop in the seasoned flour in a paper bag. Brown the chop in a little hot oil and place in a casserole. Add the onion, the apricot halves and the soy sauce. Cover and bake at 350°F/Gas Mark 4 for 30 minutes, then uncover and cook for a further 15–20 minutes.

Pork Chop in Milk

Put the chop in a small ovenproof dish and spread with a little made mustard, then sprinkle on brown sugar and season with salt. Barely cover with milk and cook in a very slow oven (or on a *low* hot plate) for about 1½ hours.

Southern Pork Chop

1 chop
Butter
1 pineapple ring
1 teaspoon flour
3 tablespoons pineapple juice
1 teaspoon tomato purée
Pinch of thyme
A little chopped onion
Salt and pepper

Brown the chop in a little butter and place in a casserole. Top the chop with a pineapple ring. Stir the flour into the pan juices and blend together. Add the pineapple juice, a small pinch of thyme, the tomato purée and the chopped onion. Stir well. Season with salt and pepper and pour over the chop. Cover and cook at 350°F/Gas Mark 4 for 40–50 minutes. Uncover for the last 15 minutes, so that the pineapple will glaze.

Pork and Corn Parcel

½ oz butter
1 teaspoon chopped onion
Pinch of chilli powder
Pinch of ground ginger
2 tablespoons drained sweetcorn
1 teaspoon chopped parsley
1 pork chump chop ¼–1 inch thick (or slice of lean pork, or pork leg steak)

Butter a square of foil slightly larger than the chop. Heat the remaining butter and fry the onion until soft but not brown, stir in the chilli powder and ginger and cook for a minute. Remove from the heat and stir in the corn and parsley. Lay the chop or the slice of pork on the foil and season well. Top with the corn mixture and fold the foil over to form a parcel, rolling the edges together. Place on an ovenproof dish and cook in a moderately hot oven (375°F/Gas Mark 5) for about 45 minutes.

Pork and Apple Parcel

1 pork chop
½ tablespoon cooking oil or margarine
Salt and pepper
1 small cooking apple, peeled and sliced
Pinch of dried sage
½ small orange

Remove rind from chop. Heat just enough oil or margarine to cover the bottom of a frying pan and fry the chop quickly on each side to brown and seal. Season with salt and pepper.

Butter a square of foil slightly larger than the chop and put the chop in the centre. Place the apple slices on top and add a pinch of sage. Squeeze the juice from the orange half over the apple. Fold up the foil loosely around the chop to form a parcel, rolling the edges together to secure firmly. Place on an ovenproof dish and cook for ¾–1 hour at 375°F/Gas Mark 5.

Spare Ribs with Orange and Ginger

¾–1 lb pork spare ribs
Dry mustard
1 teaspoon ground ginger
1 tablespoon brown sugar
2 small oranges

Cut up the spare ribs, sprinkle with a little dry mustard, place in a baking dish and roast uncovered for 30 minutes at 375°F/Gas Mark 5. Sprinkle the ground ginger and brown sugar on the spare ribs and then the juice and grated rind of one orange. Cook for a further 30–45 minutes. Slice the other orange and warm in a covered dish in the oven to serve with the spare ribs.

Spare ribs, cooked this way, are usually eaten with the fingers.

Spare Ribs with Sweet and Sour Sauce

¾–1 lb pork spare ribs
Dry mustard
1 small can pineapple slices
2 tablespoons vinegar
3 level teaspoons brown sugar or honey
1 level teaspoon tomato ketchup
Squeeze of lemon juice (optional)
½ level teaspoon ground ginger
1 teaspoon cornflour

77

2 tablespoons water
Salt and pepper

Cut up the spare ribs, sprinkle them with a little dry mustard, place in a baking dish and roast uncovered for 30 minutes at 375°F/Gas Mark 5. While the spare ribs are cooking, prepare the sweet and sour sauce. Put 2 tablespoons of the pineapple juice into a pan with the vinegar, brown sugar or honey, tomato ketchup, ginger, lemon juice and water. Bring to the boil and thicken with the cornflour. Season to taste with salt and pepper. Remove the spare ribs from the oven and pour away any fat. Then pour on the sauce and continue cooking for 45 minutes, basting occasionally. Serve with the pineapple slices, which can be warmed through in the oven, and rice.

Another finger licking dish!

Fried

Plain

Grease the pan with pork fat, and fry the chop over a moderate heat until browned on each side. Continue to cook, reducing the heat a little until cooked through (15–20 minutes).

German Style

Fry a chop until the fat runs. Turn the chop over and add a sliced onion and a peeled and sliced apple to the pan. Sprinkle with a pinch of dried mixed herbs and season with salt and pepper. Cook gently until the pork is cooked through.

BACON CHOPS

Bacon chops are really extra-thick back rashers cut from the leanest part of the back, and are available at many butchers and supermarkets. Each chop weighs approximately 6 oz. If you want the butcher to cut one specially for you, make sure it's ½ inch thick.

COOKING METHODS

Grilled

Bacon Chop with Pineapple Rice

1 small can pineapple rings or pieces
1 level tablespoon brown sugar
1 teaspoon vinegar
1 bacon chop
2 oz rice
½ oz butter

Drain the pineapple and put 4 tablespoons of the juice in a pan with the sugar and vinegar. Boil rapidly for several minutes to reduce and thicken the sauce. Place the chop under a hot grill for 3 minutes, reduce the heat and grill gently for 9–12 minutes, turning once. While the chop is grilling, cook the rice, drain it well and return it to the pan with the butter and half the pineapple pieces. Heat through and serve the chop on the rice with the sauce poured over.

Bacon Chop with Liver Sausage

Make a 2-inch long cut on the rind side of the chop and press ½ oz of liver sausage into the pouch. Brush the chop with melted margarine and grill in the usual way.

Baked

Spiced Bacon Bake

1 bacon chop
2 teaspoons cornflour
2 oz brown sugar
¼ level teaspoon dry mustard
Pinch of nutmeg
Pinch of cinnamon
2 pineapple slices, halved
2 oz mushrooms, sliced
¼ pint cider or 4 tablespoons lager

Remove excess fat from bacon chops and place side by side in a shallow casserole dish. Mix together the sugar, mustard, spices and cornflour, and sprinkle over the chops. Add the mushrooms and pineapple slices. Add the cider, or lager, cover and bake at 350°F/Gas Mark 4 for 25–30 minutes.

Bacon Chop with Orange and Sugar

1 bacon chop
1 level teaspoonful dark brown sugar
½ lb potatoes, or 1 small packet instant mashed potato
Salt and pepper
½ oz butter or margarine
Juice of ½ orange

Place the chop in a lightly greased shallow ovenproof dish. Sprinkle the sugar over the chop. Bake uncovered in the oven at 350°F/Gas Mark 4 for about 20 minutes. Turn the chop, baste, and cook for a further 20 minutes. Boil the potatoes and mash or, if using instant, make up as directed on packet. Beat in the butter or margarine, salt and pepper and orange juice. Pile on to a plate and top with the bacon chop.

Somerset Bacon Chop

1 bacon chop
1 tablespoon onion, finely chopped
Butter
½ small cooking apple, cored, peeled and grated
1 level dessertspoon fresh white breadcrumbs
½ teaspoon sultanas or raisins (optional)
A little beaten egg

With a sharp knife, cut through the bacon chop from the outside edge to within ¾ inch of the inside edge, to form a pocket. Fry the onion in a knob of butter until soft. Mix with the apple, breadcrumbs and sultanas or raisins. Season. Bind with a little beaten egg. Use this mixture to stuff the pocket in the chop. Place the chop in a roasting tin. Spoon over a little melted butter and bake in a moderately hot oven, 375°F/Gas Mark 5, for 30 minutes, basting from time to time, until the chop is golden and tender.

Fried

Plain

Remove the rind from the chop and snip the fat at intervals. Fry the meat gently or use own fat, or add a little butter, and cook for 5 minutes each side.

Crumbled Bacon Chop

Remove the rind and snip the fat at intervals. Dip the chop in a little beaten egg and then in 1 tablespoon of bread sauce crumbs or dried breadcrumbs. Fry the breaded chop gently in butter, 5 minutes each side.

4 Thirty Ways with Chicken ... and Turkey

If you tend to eat chicken once a week you'll find thirty new recipes in this chapter to help ring the changes. I've included recipes for as many parts of the chicken as possible. Most supermarkets and many butchers sell chicken livers, thighs, wings, giblets and drumsticks, so there's lots of scope. More and more shops are selling turkey pieces, and the breasts and drumsticks make excellent dishes. Appetites vary, so I've suggested 1–2 chicken pieces in the recipes – the dishes either reheat well or taste good cold, so there's a bonus in cooking extra.

Buttery Garlic Chicken

1½ oz butter
1 tablespoon malt vinegar
1 tablespoon honey
1 small garlic clove, crushed
1 level teaspoon salt
¼ level teaspoon marjoram
¼ level teaspoon dry mustard
1–2 chicken pieces

Melt the butter in a small pan over low heat. Stir in the vinegar, honey, garlic, salt, mustard and marjoram. Line the grill pan with foil and place on the chicken pieces, fleshy side upwards. Spoon over the butter and honey mixture and leave for 30–40 minutes. Turn the grill to high and cook the chicken for 5 minutes, then lower the heat and cook for another 10 minutes. Turn the chicken over and cook for 10–15 minutes, basting with the pan juices. To test if the chicken is cooked, pierce the thickest part of the flesh with a skewer or fork – if the juices run clear, the chicken is cooked and ready to eat.

Honey and Orange Chicken Grill

1–2 chicken pieces
Butter
Juice of 1 small orange
2 teaspoons honey

Dot the chicken pieces with butter, sprinkle with salt and pepper and grill under a moderate heat until cooked, 25–30 minutes, turning occasionally and basting with the pan juices. Mix the orange juice with the honey. When the chicken is cooked, pour away excess fat from the tin and pour the orange mixture over the chicken. Grill for another 5 minutes. Serve with salad.

Note
Plain grilled chicken is delicious with hot orange slices. Peel and slice a small orange, sprinkle with sugar and heat the slices for a few minutes in the buttery juices in the bottom of the grill pan.

Ginger Chicken

1–2 chicken pieces
1 tablespoon seasoned flour
1 tablespoon cooking oil
1 oz butter
1 small onion, sliced
½ teaspoon ground ginger
1 teaspoon French mustard

¼ pint chicken stock (use water and ½ stock cube)
1 tablespoon sherry

Toss the chicken in the seasoned flour in a bag. Heat the oil and butter in a frying pan and fry the chicken until brown. Remove to a small casserole. Fry the onion in the pan juices. Stir in any excess flour and the ginger and mustard. Stir in the sherry and the stock off the heat. Replace on the heat and bring to the boil, stirring. Pour over the chicken, cover and cook at 325°F/Gas Mark 3 for 1–1½ hours.

Note
Instead of the stock and sherry, ½ bottle of ginger ale can be used.

Chicken or Turkey Escalope

1 boned chicken or turkey breast
2 tablespoons fresh white breadcrumbs
2 teaspoons grated Parmesan cheese (optional)
Pinch of dried mixed herbs
½ beaten egg
1 tablespoon cooking oil
½ oz butter
Pepper

Beat out the breast using the method described in the Turkey Olive recipe (see p. 99). Mix the breadcrumbs, cheese and herbs together and season with pepper. Dip the breast in the beaten egg, drain and then coat with the crumb mixture. Heat the oil and butter in a frying pan and fry the escalope until golden brown on one side, turn over and brown the second side, 7–10 minutes altogether.

Chicken Hawaii

1–2 chicken pieces
½ oz soft margarine
1 teaspoon flour
2 teaspoons tomato ketchup
¼ teaspoon dry mustard
½ small can pineapple pieces

Place the chicken pieces in an ovenproof dish. Mix the margarine, flour, ketchup and mustard together and spread over the chicken. Pour over the pineapple syrup and the pineapple pieces. Bake at 375°F/Gas Mark 5 for 1 hour.

Roman Chicken

1–2 chicken pieces
1 tablespoon seasoned flour
1 tablespoon cooking oil
¼ pint stock (use water and ½ stock cube)
2 oz mushrooms, sliced
1 small can tomatoes
1 bay leaf
Pinch of sugar

Toss the chicken pieces in seasoned flour in a bag. Heat the oil and brown the chicken on both sides. Add the stock, mushrooms, tomatoes, bay leaf and a pinch of sugar. Season with salt and pepper. Bring to the boil, cover and simmer very gently for 1 hour.

Steamed Chicken Cream

4 oz minced chicken, cooked or raw
1 oz margarine or butter
1 bacon rasher, trimmed and diced
2 teaspoons chopped onion
1 oz flour

¼ pint milk
1 egg, lightly beaten
Salt and pepper

Melt the margarine or butter in a pan and lightly fry the
bacon and onion. Remove from the pan. Stir the flour into
the pan juices, blend well and add the milk. Bring to the
boil, stirring. Mix in the onion, bacon, chicken and beaten
egg. Season with salt and pepper. Turn into a basin and
steam for 1 hour if the chicken was raw or for 30 minutes if
the chicken was cooked.

Drumsticks Peking

1–2 chicken or turkey drumsticks
1 teaspoon soy sauce
1 oz soft butter or margarine
2 tablespoons honey

Preheat the oven to 450°F/Gas Mark 8. Mix the honey, soy
sauce and butter or margarine together, and coat each drumstick with the mixture. Place the drumsticks in an ovenproof
pan, lined with cooking foil, and bake for 45 minutes. Turn
the pieces once or twice, being careful not to pierce the skin,
and baste them with the honey and butter mixture. The
skin will go very dark and crisp. Lower the heat to 350°F/Gas
Mark 4, cover and cook until tender, 20–30 minutes.

Note
Equally good with any chicken piece.

Chicken with Orange Casserole

1–2 chicken pieces (the leg is ideal)
1 tablespoon flour
½ oz margarine or cooking oil
1 teaspoon chopped onion or ½ teaspoon dried onion
2 bacon rashers

6 tablespoons chicken stock (use water and ¼ stock cube)
Juice and grated rind of ½ small orange
1 bay leaf
Salt and pepper

Toss the chicken in the flour. Heat the margarine or oil in
a pan and brown the chicken all over. Remove the chicken.
Cook the onion and chopped bacon in the fat for 5 minutes,
stir in any excess flour and cook for another couple of minutes.
Add the stock and bring to the boil, stirring. Add the orange
rind, juice and the bay leaf and replace the chicken. Season
to taste with salt and pepper and cook for 1 hour at 325°F/
Gas Mark 3 until tender.

Note
Halve the orange before removing the rind and juice.

Crispy Chicken Bake

1 packet potato crisps
1–2 chicken pieces
Seasoned flour
1 tablespoon tomato ketchup

Crush 2 tablespoons potato crisps with a rolling pin. Dip the
chicken pieces in a little seasoned flour to coat and then
brush with the tomato ketchup. Coat with the crushed
potato crisps, place skin side up on a lightly greased baking
dish and cook for 40 minutes in a preheated oven 400°F/Gas
Mark 6. Serve with the rest of the potato crisps.
Equally good hot or cold.

Variation
The chicken joint can also be dipped in evaporated milk and
coated with coarse breadcrumbs.

Chicken Maryland

1–2 chicken joints (frying chicken)
1 egg, lightly beaten
2–3 tablespoons breadcrumbs
1 tablespoon seasoned flour
2 tablespoons cooking fat or oil
1 banana
1 bacon rasher, cut in strips (optional)

Coat the chicken lightly with the seasoned flour, shaking off any excess, dip in lightly beaten egg and coat with bread-crumbs. Fry quickly in the hot fat or oil ($\frac{1}{2}$ inch deep) until golden brown on both sides, turning once. Reduce the heat and cook gently, uncovered, until tender, 15–20 minutes. After cooking the chicken, drain off most of the fat. Slice the banana in half lengthways, sprinkle with flour and fry in the hot fat with the bacon strips for a couple of minutes.

Note
Sweetcorn fritters are another good accompaniment.

Spiced Chicken and Apricots

1–2 chicken pieces (the leg is ideal)
1 large can apricots
1 tablespoon seasoned flour
2 tablespoons cooking oil
$\frac{1}{2}$ small onion, finely chopped
$\frac{1}{4}$ level teaspoon curry powder
2 teaspoons lemon juice
1 clove (optional)
6 tablespoons chicken stock (use water and $\frac{1}{4}$ stock cube)

Drain the apricots, keep 3 tablespoons of juice and 6 apricots for this recipe and put the rest aside to eat tomorrow. Slice the six apricots. Coat the chicken with seasoned flour. Heat the oil in a frying pan and brown the chicken pieces on all sides. Remove to a small casserole. Cook the onion in the pan juices until it begins to brown. Stir in the rest of the flour, curry powder, sliced apricots and juice, lemon juice, clove and chicken stock, and bring to the boil, stirring. Pour over the chicken, cover and cook at 325°F/Gas Mark 3 for 1¼ hours, until tender.

Chicken in a Pot

1 oz butter or margarine
2 carrots, sliced
1 medium onion, sliced
2 rashers streaky bacon, derinded and diced
Pinch of thyme
1 small bay leaf
Salt and pepper
1–2 chicken pieces
1 small packet mashed potato
1–2 tablespoons grated cheese

Heat the butter or margarine in an ovenproof casserole which is just large enough to hold the chicken and vegetables, and cook the carrots, onion and bacon for 10 minutes. Add the chicken pieces, thyme and bay leaf, and season lightly with salt and pepper. Cover and cook in a slow oven, 300°F/Gas Mark 2, for 1–1½ hours. At the end of cooking, make up the mashed potato topping, spread it over the top, sprinkle with grated cheese and brown under a low grill.

Note
A small crushed garlic clove or a little grated lemon rind can be added to the seasoning.

Chicken and Mushroom Risotto

½ small onion, chopped
½ oz margarine
3–4 oz raw chicken livers, chopped

2 oz rice
⅓ pint chicken stock (use water and ½ stock cube)
2 oz mushrooms
1 tablespoon grated cheese

Heat the margarine in a pan and fry the onion until soft. Add the chopped chicken livers and rice and stir for several minutes. Pour on the stock and bring to the boil. Cover and simmer gently for 20–25 minutes until the liquid has been absorbed. Sauté the mushrooms in a knob of margarine for 2–3 minutes and, when the rice is cooked, stir it into the mixture together with the grated cheese.

Curried Chicken

1–2 chicken pieces
2 tablespoons cooking oil
1 small onion, sliced
1 small apple, sliced
1–2 level teaspoons curry powder (according to taste)
1 teaspoon flour
4 tablespoons chicken stock (use water and ¼ stock cube)
1 level teaspoon tomato purée
1 level teaspoon mango chutney
2 teaspoons raisins
1 tablespoon smooth peanut butter (optional)

Fry the chicken pieces in the oil until lightly browned and then remove from the pan. Fry the onion and the apple in the pan juices for 5 minutes. Stir in the curry powder, cook for a few minutes and then sprinkle on the flour. Add the stock, tomato purée, mango chutney and raisins. Replace the chicken pieces in the pan and simmer gently for 30–40 minutes. Stir in the peanut butter. Serve with plain boiled rice and salted peanuts or crisps.

Notes
Peas, diced celery or a can of carrots can be added to the curry.

One quick salad which goes well with curry can be made by mixing finely grated raw carrot with dessicated coconut and lemon juice.

A tablespoon of natural yogurt stirred into the curry when serving will make the curry taste milder.

Chicken Livers – Chinese Style

4 oz chopped raw chicken livers
1 level tablespoon cornflour
½ level teaspoon ground ginger
½ level teaspoon salt
1 level teaspoon yeast extract (or 1 tablespoon soy sauce)
2 tablespoons cooking sherry
2 tablespoons cooking oil

Put the cornflour, ginger, salt, yeast extract and sherry in a bowl and stir in the chicken livers. Heat the oil in a frying pan, add the liver mixture and cook for 3 minutes over a moderate heat, stirring with the handle of a wooden spoon. Serve with boiled rice.

Fried Drumsticks with Barbecue Sauce

1–2 chicken or turkey drumsticks
1 egg
1 tablespoon bread sauce mix
2 tablespoons sage and onion stuffing mix
Cooking oil or fat for deep frying

Barbecue Sauce
2 tablespoons tomato sauce or ketchup
1 teaspoon Worcester sauce
1 teaspoon vinegar
½ teaspoon made mustard

Mix the bread sauce mix and sage and onion stuffing mix together. Dip the drumsticks into the beaten egg and then coat in the bread and stuffing mixture. Fry in deep hot fat for 15 minutes, turning occasionally. Mix all the sauce ingredients together in a small bowl and serve with the drumsticks.

Notes

There is no need to deep fry in a *large* frying pan – you can manage very successfully with any small, thick-bottomed saucepan which will hold the drumsticks. (See the notes on Frying Temperatures (p. 45) to judge the right heat.) After frying, leave the oil to cool down and, when quite cold, strain through a sieve into a screw-top jar. Leave in a cool place, ready to use again. *Never* strain hot oil.

Chicken Breast with Ham and Cheese

1 boned chicken breast
Seasoned flour
1 oz butter
4 tablespoons hot chicken stock (use water and $\frac{1}{4}$ stock cube)
Pinch of oregano
3–4 sliced mushrooms
1 slice cooked ham
1 slice cheddar cheese

Skin the chicken breast and lightly coat with the flour. Melt the butter in a pan and fry the chicken breast for a minute on each side. Add the hot chicken stock, mushrooms and a pinch of oregano. Cover and simmer for 20 minutes. Place a slice of cooked ham on the chicken, then add a layer of the mushrooms and top with the cheese. Cover again and cook until the cheese melts.

Note

More, or even less, mushrooms can be used, or they can be omitted altogether.

Cold Chicken with Yogurt Sauce

1–2 chicken drumsticks
Plain flour
1 egg, beaten
2 tablespoons bread sauce mix
Cooking oil or fat for deep frying

Yogurt Sauce
½ carton natural yogurt
1 teaspoon lemon juice
Pinch of cayenne pepper (optional)
1 teaspoon chopped chives (fresh or dried) or parsley

Toss the chicken drumsticks in the flour, then dip them in the beaten egg and finally coat them with the dry bread sauce mix. Fry in hot deep fat for 15–20 minutes until the crumbs are golden brown and the chicken is thoroughly cooked. Drain well. Mix the sauce ingredients together and serve the chicken cold with the yogurt sauce.

Nutty Chicken

1–2 chicken pieces
½ oz margarine
½ small onion, chopped
¼ teaspoon dried mixed herbs
½ oz (1 heaped tablespoon) plain flour
2 oz crunchy peanut butter
½ pint milk

Topping
1 oz salted peanuts
1 oz fresh white breadcrumbs

Brown the chicken in the hot fat. Transfer to a casserole. Fry the onions in the fat until soft. Add the herbs and flour to the onions and cook for 2–3 minutes. Stir in the peanut butter and mix well. Remove from the heat. Add the milk, bring to the boil and stir until thick. Pour the sauce over the chicken, cover and cook for 40 minutes at 375°F/Gas Mark 5. Remove the lid and sprinkle the top with nuts and breadcrumbs. Bake for a further 10 minutes.

Chicken Paprika

1–2 chicken pieces
½ oz butter or margarine
1 small onion, finely chopped
1 level teaspoon paprika
2 tomatoes, quartered
¼ pint stock (use water and ½ stock cube)
1–2 tablespoons sour cream or plain yogurt
Salt and pepper

Brown the chicken in the hot fat. Remove from the pan. Fry the onion in the pan juices for 5 minutes. Stir in the paprika and mix well. Add the tomatoes to the pan with the stock and chicken. Season lightly with salt and pepper. Bring to the boil, cover and simmer for 45 minutes. Stir in the sour cream or yogurt. Serve with noodles.

Note
½ small green pepper, thinly sliced, could be added 10 minutes before serving.

Chicken and Asparagus

1–2 chicken leg portions
Plain flour
½ oz butter
1 tablespoonful oil
1 small can condensed asparagus soup
3 tablespoons water
2 chopped tomatoes
1 (2 oz) can baby mushrooms, drained, or 2 oz fresh mushrooms
Few drops soy sauce

96

Cut each chicken portion into two and dust with plain, unseasoned flour. Heat the butter and oil in a frying pan and brown the chicken pieces on all sides. Remove from the pan. Pour off most of the fat in the pan and then stir in the soup, water and tomatoes. Return the chicken, cover and cook gently over a low heat until tender – about 30 minutes. Arrange the chicken in a serving dish and keep hot. Add the soy sauce and mushrooms to the chicken sauce. Stir well and bring to the boil. Pour over the chicken.

Notes

If using fresh mushrooms, slice them very thinly first.

Condensed soups make very good sauces. For a very delicious creamy sauce, try condensed mushroom soup gently heated with 1–2 tablespoons single cream and a few sliced mushrooms. Very good with fish too!

Chicken Spare Ribs

1 lb chicken wings
1½ tablespoons soy sauce
3 tablespoons honey
Butter or margarine

Wash and dry the chicken wings and put them on a plate. Mix the soy sauce and honey and pour over the chicken wings. Leave at room temperature for at least 30 minutes, but the longer the better, turning occasionally. Preheat the oven to 400°F/Gas Mark 6. Grease a baking tray or oven-proof dish with the butter or margarine. Place the chicken wings flat, not overlapping, in the dish. Spoon over the marinade. Bake for 45 minutes, turning and basting every 15 minutes.

Chicken Livers with Bacon and Sage

1 bacon rasher, derinded and cut in cubes
Butter
4 oz chicken livers, cut in pieces
¼ teaspoon dried sage

Cook the bacon pieces over a moderate heat for several minutes until the fat starts to run. Add a knob of butter, raise the heat and, when the butter is foaming, add the chicken livers, salt, pepper and sage. Cook for 3–5 minutes, stirring.

Note
If you have any sherry handy, remove the cooked chicken livers and the bacon to a plate and add a dash of sherry and a similar amount of water to the pan and allow it to sizzle for a minute or two. Pour over the liver.

Chicken Pâté

1 small onion, finely chopped
2 oz butter
4 oz chicken livers
1 tablespoon brandy, sherry or port (optional)
¼ teaspoon curry powder
½ teaspoon paprika

Melt the butter in a pan, without browning, add the chopped onion and cook over a low heat until soft and transparent. While the onion is cooking, chop the chicken livers into small pieces. Add to the pan with the alcohol and cook, stirring all the time. When the livers are cooked and very soft – about 5 minutes – remove from the heat. Add the curry powder and paprika and mash until the mixture is smooth. Turn into a little dish, cover and leave in a cool place.

Notes
This is quite delicious with hot toast and butter.
The pâté will keep in the refrigerator for 3 days.

Lemon Chicken with Bacon and Mushrooms

1–2 chicken pieces
Juice of ½ lemon
1 oz butter or margarine
Salt
1 bacon rasher, derinded and cut in strips
2 oz mushrooms, sliced

Sprinkle the chicken pieces with lemon juice. Melt the butter or margarine and brush some over the chicken. Season with salt. Put the chicken skin side down in the grill pan and cook at a medium heat for 10 minutes. Turn the chicken over, brush with butter and continue grilling for 15–20 minutes, basting with the buttery juices. Heat the remaining butter or margarine in a small pan and fry the bacon and mushrooms. Squeeze on any remaining lemon juice. Serve the chicken on a warm plate with the mushrooms and bacon.

Turkey Olive

1 boned turkey breast
2 level tablespoons sage and onion stuffing
1 teaspoon lemon juice
Little grated lemon rind – if possible
2 level teaspoons chopped parsley (optional)
Pinch of ground ginger
½ oz butter or margarine
½ can (10½-oz size) cream of chicken soup

The turkey breast must first be beaten out and flattened. The easiest way is to put the turkey breast into a polythene bag or between two pieces of waxed paper, foil or wet greaseproof paper and beat with a rolling pin until thin. If you can't be bothered with the paper or bag, beat it with a wet rolling pin or wooden mallet.

Put the stuffing mix in a bowl and add 3 tablespoons boiling water. Add the lemon juice, rind, parsley and ginger and leave to stand for 10 minutes. Place the stuffing on the turkey breast, roll up and tie with cotton. Heat the butter or margarine and brown the turkey olive on all sides for 6–8 minutes. Stir in the soup, bring to the boil and simmer, covered, for 10–15 minutes.

Turkey Breast in Foil

1 boned turkey breast
2 oz chopped mushrooms
Grated onion or onion powder
2 teaspoons breadcrumbs
Butter
Salt and pepper
3 tablespoons stock (use water and $\frac{1}{4}$ stock cube)

Beat out the turkey breast as in the Turkey Olive recipe. Melt a knob of butter in a pan and fry the mushrooms and onion. Add the breadcrumbs and season with salt and pepper. Cover the turkey breast with the stuffing, roll up, tie with cotton to hold together and place on a lightly buttered piece of foil, large enough to make a parcel of the meat. Sprinkle the turkey with stock and secure the edges of the foil. Place the parcel on a baking tray or in an ovenproof dish and cook at 375°F/Gas Mark 5 for 1 hour.

Devilled Turkey Drumsticks

2 level teaspoons chutney, chopped
1 teaspoon tomato ketchup
Generous pinch of mustard powder
Generous pinch of mixed spice
3 tablespoons fresh breadcrumbs
Salt and pepper
Dash of Worcester sauce (optional)
1–2 turkey drumsticks
1 oz margarine

Mix the chutney, ketchup, mustard and spice with 1 table-spoon of the breadcrumbs. Season with salt and pepper and add the Worcester sauce. Make three or four deep slits in the turkey flesh and fill each with some of the devilled mixture. Cover and leave in a cool place for an hour or so. Place the drumsticks in a baking dish or roasting pan and pour over a little melted margarine. Brown the remaining breadcrumbs in hot margarine and sprinkle on top. Cook, covered, in a hot oven, 400°F/Gas Mark 6, for 40 minutes. Uncover and continue cooking for a further 30 minutes.

Notes
It is worth cooking an extra drumstick to eat cold the next day with salad.

Packet bread sauce or stuffing mix can be substituted for fresh breadcrumbs.

Oven-fried Chicken

1 tablespoon flour
1 tablespoon grated Parmesan cheese
¼ teaspoon curry powder
¼ teaspoon salt
½ oz butter
1–2 chicken pieces

Preheat the oven to 425°F/Gas Mark 7. Shake together the flour, cheese, salt and curry powder in a paper bag. Melt the butter in a shallow baking tin in the oven, dip the chicken pieces in it and then coat them evenly with the cheese mixture. Place the chicken pieces, skin side down, in the baking tin. Cook uncovered for 20 minutes, then turn the chicken skin side up and continue cooking for a further 10 minutes or until golden brown and tender.

5 More Meat Meals

Moving away from chops and chicken, there are lots of meats which are economical for the single person. And there's no reason why cooking for one should exclude joints of meat. You can make the most of your oven time, too, by cooking your vegetables alongside your meat – braised vegetables are lovely. Or you can try baking whole onions or tomatoes French style. If you have never cooked things like tripe or tongue, have a go with these recipes, which are simple to follow and really quite delicious.

Crispy Pork Fillet

4 oz pork fillet
Seasoned flour
1 egg, lightly beaten
Breadcrumbs
1 oz butter

Trim away any fat from the outside of the fillet and cut the meat into two thick pieces. Place each one, one at a time, cut side down between two sheets of dampened greaseproof paper (this prevents the meat sticking to the paper) or in a polythene bag, and beat flat with a rolling pin. Dip the flattened pieces of meat in seasoned flour and then in the beaten egg. Finally coat with breadcrumbs, patting them on firmly. Heat the butter in a frying pan and fry the meat over a medium heat for 5–6 minutes, turning to brown both sides evenly. Drain well.

Mixed Grill

2–3 mushrooms
1 small lamb chop or a piece of pork spare rib
1–2 sausages
1 rasher bacon
1 tomato

Rinse the mushrooms under running water and dry with a cloth or kitchen paper. Preheat the grill. Place the chop and sausages on the greased grill rack and turn after 5–7 minutes. Add the bacon, halved tomato and mushrooms, and grill for a further 5–7 minutes.

Ham Steak with Grilled Apple Rings

1 ham steak
Cooking oil
Salt and pepper
Brown sugar
1 apple

Brush the ham steak with a little oil and season with salt and pepper. Grill for 3–5 minutes, turn over and spread with a thick layer of brown sugar. Grill until the sugar melts, reducing the heat so that the sugar does not burn. Core and slice the apple, sprinkle with brown sugar and grill beside the ham for a couple of minutes, turning once.

Note
If you have an extra ham steak, serve it fried the next day with an egg on top.

Baked Ham Rolls

With Parsley and Thyme Stuffing and Apple

2 level tablespoons parsley and thyme or sage and onion
    stuffing mix
3 tablespoons boiling water
1 egg
1 small apple, cored and chopped (but not peeled unless you
    prefer to)
½ teaspoon dried mixed herbs
Salt and pepper
3 slices cooked ham
¼ pint hot cheese sauce, homemade, or ½ packet cheese
    sauce mix

Put the stuffing mix in a bowl and pour on the boiling water. Stir in the egg, chopped apple and herbs, and season well with salt and pepper. Leave to stand for 10 minutes. Divide the stuffing among the ham slices and form into rolls. Place close together in an ovenproof dish. Pour the hot cheese sauce over the ham rolls and bake at 375°F/Gas Mark 5 for 20 minutes.

With Banana and Chutney

1 tablespoon sweet chutney
1 banana
2 slices ham
¼ pint hot cheese sauce

Spread the ham slices with chutney. Peel the banana and cut in two. Roll a slice of ham round each piece of banana and place in a small ovenproof dish. Pour over the hot cheese sauce. A little extra grated cheese can be sprinkled on top. Bake at 375°F/Gas Mark 5 for 20 minutes.

Note
Instead of the cheese sauce, mix ⅓ can condensed cream of mushroom soup with 2 tablespoons each of milk and grated cheese. Spoon over the ham rolls.

With Celery

1 can celery hearts – drain and put 2 aside to have as an extra vegetable tomorrow
2–3 slices ham
¼ pint cheese sauce
2 tablespoons grated cheese
1 tablespoon dried breadcrumbs or bread sauce mix

Wrap each celery heart in a slice of ham and place in an ovenproof dish. Make the cheese sauce and pour it over the ham. Sprinkle with 1 tablespoon of the grated cheese and bake at 350°F/Gas Mark 4 for 15 minutes. Mix the remaining grated cheese with the breadcrumbs or dry bread sauce mix. Sprinkle over the dish. Return to the oven for a further 5–10 minutes to brown slightly.

Hamburger with Barbecue Sauce

4 oz minced beef
1 teaspoon grated or dried onion
Salt and pepper
Worcester sauce

Barbecue Sauce
1 teaspoon honey or syrup
1 tablespoon tomato ketchup
1 tablespoon Worcester sauce
1 teaspoon vinegar
1 teaspoon water
½ oz margarine or 2 teaspoons cooking oil
1 teaspoon grated onion

Mix the beef and onion. Season with salt and pepper and a dash of Worcester sauce. Form into one large or two small hamburgers and grill for about 10 minutes each side. Pour on the barbecue sauce.

To prepare the sauce: Put all the ingredients for the sauce in a small pan and heat gently.

Note
For an American hamburger, split and toast a bun. Spread the bun with mustard and pop the hamburger inside.

Savoury Meat Loaf

8 oz fresh minced beef
1 bacon rasher, derinded and chopped
2 tablespoons grated onion
1 teacup breadcrumbs or 1–2 slices of bread, soaked in milk or water and squeezed dry
2 tablespoons evaporated milk or 1 tablespoon Marvel
1 tablespoon thick gravy (optional)
2 teaspoons finely chopped parsley (optional)
Salt and pepper

slowly, cover and simmer for 2–2½ hours until the bones slip out easily. Remove the bones. Flatten the meat by putting it between two plates and placing a weight on top. Leave to cool. Dip the trotters in the beaten egg, roll them in the breadcrumbs and fry in the hot fat until golden.

Farmhouse Meatballs

2 rashers streaky bacon
2 pork sausages or 3 oz sausagemeat
Pinch of dried mixed herbs
2 oz fresh white breadcrumbs
Salt and pepper
2 oz pig's or lamb's liver, finely chopped
2–3 tablespoons dried breadcrumbs or flour
2 tablespoons cooking oil

Remove the bacon rind and cut the bacon into small pieces. Skin the sausages and mix together with the bacon, mixed herbs and fresh breadcrumbs. Season well with salt and pepper. Divide the mixture in half. Shape each half into a round, putting the chopped liver into the centre and fold over to enclose. Flatten the meatballs slightly and coat with dried breadcrumbs or flour. Heat the oil in a pan and fry the meatballs over a medium heat for 10–12 minutes each side until cooked right through. Serve with spaghetti or mashed potato.

Bacon Rolls in Kidney and Tomato Sauce

1 level tablespoon sage and onion stuffing mix
1 tablespoon boiling water
2 lamb's kidneys
1 small onion, sliced
1 tablespoon cooking oil
2 rashers streaky bacon
2 level teaspoons plain flour
½ can (5½-oz size) condensed tomato soup
2 tablespoons water

Put the stuffing in a cup, pour on the water, mix and leave to stand for 10 minutes. Slice the kidneys, removing the core. Remove the bacon rinds and stretch the rashers, using the back of a knife. Divide the stuffing between the rashers and roll the bacon around it. Fry the onion in the hot oil until soft and then put the kidneys and bacon rolls into the pan. Cook over a moderate heat, turning the bacon rolls and kidney slices, for about 10 minutes. Remove the bacon rolls and keep them hot. Stir the flour into the pan and then add the soup and water. Bring to the boil, stirring all the time. Cook for 2 minutes. Serve with the bacon rolls.

Continental Kidneys

2 lamb's kidneys
½ oz margarine or lard
1 small onion, thinly sliced
2 oz mushrooms, sliced
1 level tablespoon flour
¼ pint beef stock (use water and ½ stock cube)
1 teaspoon tomato purée
2 tablespoons natural yogurt with a squeeze of lemon juice.
  or sour cream
2 oz macaroni or rice
Salt

Cut the kidneys in half, remove the fat and skin. Slit in half on the rounded side and, with a sharp knife or kitchen scissors, snip out all the centre core. Melt the margarine or lard in a pan and cook the onion slices over a low heat until soft. Add the mushrooms to the pan and cook for a couple of minutes. Add the kidneys and fry for 3–4 minutes. Stir in the flour, stock and tomato purée. Bring to the boil and simmer gently for 10 minutes. Cook the macaroni or rice in fast-boiling salted water for 12–15 minutes and drain well. Place on a warm plate and pour on the kidney mixture. Spoon the yogurt or sour cream on top.

Notes

Kidneys are also excellent cooked in their own fat. Put them whole into a small ovenproof dish or baking tin and bake at 350°F/Gas Mark 4 for 30 minutes. Cut off the fat, season them with salt and pepper and return to the oven for 5 minutes.

If kidneys are grilled, always brush them first with oil or melted margarine – this stops the skin from hardening on the outside.

Lamb's kidneys are ideal for grills, sautés and braises.

Pig's kidneys are very tasty but have a stronger flavour and should be soaked in milk for about half an hour before cooking. Ox kidney has a very strong flavour and is traditionally used only in puddings and pies.

Curried Liver and Kidney

1–2 lamb's kidneys
4 oz liver
½ oz butter
¼ teaspoon curry powder
½ teaspoon made mustard
Generous pinch of salt
1 rounded tablespoon flour
4 tablespoons stock or water

Skin and core the kidneys as explained in the recipe for Continental Kidneys. Slice the kidneys and the liver. Melt the butter in a pan, stir in the curry powder, mustard and salt, and fry for 5 minutes. Add the meat and fry for 2–3 minutes. Stir in the flour, then the stock. Cover and simmer for 10 minutes.

Liver with Lemon and Herbs

3 oz pig's or lamb's liver
1 tablespoon seasoned cornflour
1 level tablespoon sugar
½ teaspoon dried mixed herbs
Juice of 1 small lemon
2 tablespoons cooking oil

Slice the liver as thinly as possible or cut into matchsticks if this is easier. Mix in a bowl with the cornflour, herbs, lemon juice and sugar. Fry the liver quickly in the hot oil, stirring with the handle of a wooden spoon. Serve in a ring of savoury rice (2 oz cooked rice mixed with 2 oz grated cheese and chopped tomato).

Notes

Never *overcook* liver as it will become tough.

To make the liver easier to slice, pour a cup of boiling water over it and leave it for 1 minute, then drain.

A few salted peanuts can be sprinkled on top.

Liver and Bacon Scramble

1 rasher streaky bacon, trimmed
½ teaspoon dried onion
4 oz liver, sliced
Knob of butter
2 eggs, lightly beaten
2 teaspoons milk

Fry the bacon in its own fat for several minutes. Add the onion and liver and fry gently until the liver is tender. Melt the butter in a separate pan. Mix the beaten eggs with milk, salt and pepper and scramble slowly in the butter. Add the scrambled eggs to the liver and bacon in the frying pan and mix lightly together. Serve with hot buttered toast.

Roast Lamb with Parsnips

A best end of neck of lamb is an ideal small roasting joint – the 5–7 chops allowing for a hot and a cold meal.

Rub the fat with a teaspoon of cooking oil and sprinkle on salt and a little dried rosemary or a few dried mixed herbs. Roast at 375°F/Gas Mark 5 for ¾–1 hour, according to how pink you like your meat. Peel 2 parsnips, cut in thick slices and boil in lightly salted water for 5–10 minutes. Drain and roast for 30–40 minutes in the pan with the lamb. Swedes or, of course, potatoes can be roasted instead of parsnips.

Notes

For a delicious shiny glaze for the lamb, cut away as much fat as possible, mix 1 tablespoon honey with orange juice and spread over the lamb before cooking, basting every so often. For a crusty outside, mix together 2 tablespoons soft white breadcrumbs mixed with ¼ teaspoon thyme and ½ teaspoon rosemary, salt and freshly ground pepper. Spread this mixture on top of the honey glaze, pressing it down firmly with the palm of the hand. Baste occasionally during cooking.

Garlic adds extra flavour to lamb. With a sharp pointed knife, make a few incisions in the skin about 2 inches apart. Peel a clove of garlic and cut into thin slivers. Insert a sliver of garlic into each incision, pressing it down well until out of sight. Roast in the usual way.

Stuffed Breast of Lamb

1 breast of lamb
Salt and pepper
Flour
Cooking fat
1 onion, chopped
1 carrot, chopped
Stock (use water and a stock cube)

One of the nicest ways of eating a small breast of lamb is boned and stuffed, and some supermarkets and butchers sell them ready-boned and rolled. (If you can't buy them ready-prepared, remove the bones carefully with a small sharp knife.) Spread on the stuffing, roll the meat up and tie with string. Season with salt and pepper and dust with flour. Melt a little fat in a pan and cook the onion and carrot for 10 minutes over a low heat. Add the meat and brown it carefully on all sides. Remove the meat and add just enough stock to the pan to barely cover the vegetables. Bring to the boil, replace the meat, cover and simmer gently either on top of the stove or in the oven at 300°F/Gas Mark 2. Allow 25 minutes to the pound and 25 minutes over. Remove the meat and skim off any fat in the pan. Stir 1 rounded teaspoon cornflower or gravy mix into the remaining pan juices to make gravy.

For a crisper finish to the joint, cover the pan and cook on the top shelf of the oven at 300°F/Gas Mark 2 for 1 hour. Remove the lid, shake over some seasoned flour and baste with the fat. Cook for another $\frac{1}{2}$ hour or until brown and crisp. Pour off the fat and stir the blended gravy mix into the remaining pan juices (1 teaspoon powder to $\frac{1}{4}$ pint water).

Stuffings

SAUSAGEMEAT AND APRICOT. Chop 2 oz dried apricots, which have been soaked overnight, and mix with 4 oz sausagemeat and 1 oz (7 level tablespoons) fresh breadcrumbs. Add a little chopped onion and season with salt and pepper.

POTATO AND HERB. Mash 1–2 large boiled potatoes with a little fat. Add a teaspoon of finely chopped onion and $\frac{1}{2}$ level teaspoon dried mixed herbs.

RICE AND RAISIN. Mix a cup of cooked rice with 1 level tablespoon raisins or sultanas, some grated onion and the juice of $\frac{1}{2}$ small lemon. The lemon rind can also be added.

SAUSAGEMEAT AND BREADCRUMBS. Mix 4 oz sausagemeat with 2 oz fresh or dried breadcrumbs and moisten with stock or water. Season well.

ONION AND SWEETCORN. Melt a knob of butter or margarine and fry a little chopped onion until soft. Add 1 small can sweetcorn, well drained, 2 tablespoons breadcrumbs and bind with a small lightly beaten egg.

SAUSAGE AND KIDNEY. Mix 4 oz sausagemeat with a cored and chopped lamb's kidney. Season well.

APPLE AND CHUTNEY. Mix together 1 tablespoon chutney, 2 tablespoons shredded apple, $\frac{1}{2}$ finely chopped onion, 1 oz breadcrumbs and a little melted margarine.

Note
The lamb can also be cut into 4-inch pieces and each piece rolled up with stuffing – like a Swiss Roll. There is no need to tie the rolls if they are packed tightly together in a small baking dish or casserole.

To cook a breast of lamb without boning or stuffing

Cut 2–3 potatoes into thick slices, place in a greased baking dish or roasting tin, sprinkle with salt and pour over a little water. Place the meat on top and dot with dripping. Cover and cook at 325°F/Gas Mark 3 for 1 hour, then uncover and cook for 30 minutes.

Bacon Patties

Minced bacon
Mashed potato
Worcester sauce
Mustard
1 egg, beaten
Breadcrumbs, toasted
Cooking fat

Combine equal quantities of minced bacon and cooked mashed potato (fresh or instant). Season well and add a little made mustard and Worcester sauce. Shape into patties, dip in the beaten egg and toasted breadcrumbs, and fry in the hot fat until crisp.

Note
Canned corned beef can be used instead of bacon.

Baked Glazed Bacon

1 small smoked forehock joint (1–1½ lbs)
1 onion
1 carrot
1 bay leaf
6 peppercorns
Brown sugar
Fresh breadcrumbs

Soak the bacon joint in cold water overnight. Place the joint in a saucepan and cover with fresh cold water. Add the peeled onion, chopped carrot, bay leaf and peppercorns. Bring to the boil, cover and simmer for 1 hour. Test the bacon to see if it is cooked by pushing in a skewer. If it goes in and out easily, then the bacon is ready. Lift the bacon out of the pan, remove the skin and place the joint in a roasting tin. With a sharp knife, score the fat in squares or diamonds. Cover the surface with equal quantities of brown sugar and fresh breadcrumbs and bake for 20 minutes in a preheated, fairly hot oven, 375°F/Gas Mark 5. The joint will have a sweet, brown crust. The bacon is very good hot or cold.

Notes
The top can also be studded with a few cloves.

The bacon stock can be used for making soups. Take a packet of soup – lentil or tomato – and make it up with ½ bacon stock, ½ water. *Or* cook 4 oz lentils (dry) or dried peas or beans (soaked overnight) in the stock till soft – about

¾ hour. Stir in ½ can of tomatoes and thicken by stirring in 2 teaspoons cornflour which have been blended with water to a cream. Season to taste.

Three Bacon Glazes

CIDER GLAZE. Put a clove in each square or diamond and sprinkle on 2 tablespoons demerara sugar. Pour a teacup of sweet cider over the joint and bake at 375°F/Gas Mark 5 for 20–30 minutes, basting frequently.

TREACLE GLAZE. Mix 1 tablespoon each of plain flour, demerara sugar and golden syrup with 2 tablespoons of the warm bacon stock. Spread over the bacon and bake at 400°F/Gas Mark 6 for 20 minutes, basting occasionally.

SUGAR AND GINGER GLAZE. Score the bacon fat into squares and stud with cloves. Mix ½ level teaspoon powdered cloves with 1 tablespoon brown sugar and add ginger ale to make a smooth paste. Spread on the bacon and bake at 400°F/Gas Mark 6 for 20 minutes.

Bacon Cooked in Beer

1–½ lb piece bacon
1 small onion
1 bay leaf
1 carrot
½ pint light or brown ale

Put the bacon into a pan with the peeled onion, bay leaf, carrot and ale. Bring to the boil, cover and cook for 1 hour. Strain the cooking liquid into a separate pan and bring back to the boil; cook hard until reduced to half the quantity. Remove the bacon rind, pour over the sauce and serve hot with green vegetables. Serve the remaining bacon cold with a green salad or use it to make a risotto.

Bacon Pudding

2 oz self-raising flour
Pinch of dry mustard
1 oz suet
2–3 rashers streaky bacon, chopped
1 small onion, chopped
Salt and pepper
1 egg, well beaten

Mix together the flour, mustard, suet, bacon and onion. Season with salt and pepper. Add sufficient well-beaten egg to make a soft dropping consistency. Turn into a small greased pudding basin, cover with greaseproof paper or foil and steam for 1 hour. Serve with fried tomatoes.

Gammon and Vegetable Risotto

1 oz butter
½ onion, peeled and chopped
1 small clove of garlic, crushed (optional)
2 oz rice
¼ pint stock (use water and ½ stock cube)
Pinch of nutmeg (optional)
Salt and pepper
2 tablespoons cooked or canned peas
½ small red or green pepper, chopped
1 small can sweetcorn, drained
2–3 oz cooked gammon, chopped or diced
2 tablespoons grated cheese

Melt the butter in a pan and cook the onion with the garlic until the onion is soft. Add the rice and cook, stirring for 4–5 minutes until transparent. Take the saucepan off the heat and add the stock and nutmeg, and season with salt and pepper. Bring slowly to the boil, stirring all the time. Cover and simmer very gently for about 20 minutes, or until all the liquid has been absorbed. Add the vegetables and bacon and cook very gently for 5 minutes. Just before serving, mix in the cheese and a little extra butter.

Notes

Instead of gammon, cooked bacon, pork, ham or chicken can be used.

A few dried apricots, cut in small pieces, go nicely with a pork risotto.

Spiced Gammon Steak

½ level teaspoon ground ginger
2 level teaspoons brown sugar
1 teaspoon Worcester sauce
1 tablespoon lemon juice
¼ teaspoon dry mustard
1 gammon steak

Mix together the ginger, sugar, Worcester sauce, lemon juice and mustard. Brush over the gammon on both sides and place in a lightly oiled, shallow, ovenproof dish. Pour over any remaining sauce and cook uncovered at 375°F/Gas Mark 5 for 30 minutes, basting occasionally.

A few canned apricot halves, well drained, can be added to the dish halfway through and basted with the sauce.

Gammon and Pineapple

Gammon and pineapple make a good combination.

Snip the rind of a gammon steak at 1-inch intervals round the steak. Brush one side with butter and pineapple syrup (from a can of pineapple rings). Grill for 5 minutes under a moderate heat. Turn over, brush the other side with butter and syrup, and grill for 15 minutes. For the last 5 minutes, grill the pineapple rings, brushed with butter and sprinkled with sugar.

Or cook the gammon, place a pineapple ring on top and cover with sliced cheese. Cook until the cheese is golden brown and melting.

Sausage Maryland with Sweetcorn Fritters

½ oz margarine
3–4 small pork sausages
½ small can sweetcorn
3 level tablespoons self-raising flour
1 tablespoon water
Salt and pepper
1 banana

Heat the margarine in a pan and fry the sausage for 10–12 minutes, turning frequently until golden brown. While they are cooking, put the drained sweetcorn with 1 tablespoon of the liquor, the flour and 1 tablespoon water into a bowl. Season with salt and pepper and mix thoroughly. When the sausages are cooked, remove them from the pan and keep warm. Place 2 or 3 tablespoons of the corn mixture into the hot fat, keeping them apart, and cook until golden brown on one side; turn and cook the other side. Drain on crumpled kitchen paper. Slice the banana in half lengthways, sprinkle with flour and fry lightly on both sides. Serve the sausages on a warm plate with the bananas and corn fritters.

Sausage and Apple

4 oz pork, or pork and beef, sausagemeat
1 teaspoon finely chopped onion
1 tablespoon chopped apple, cooking or eating
Salt and pepper
Lard or cooking oil

Mix the sausagemeat with the onion and the apple. Season with salt and pepper. Shape into two rounds ½ inch thick and fry in the hot lard or oil for 5 minutes on each side.

Sausage Supper

1 breakfast cup mashed potato, fresh or instant
1 level tablespoon flour
1 teaspoon soft margarine
1 small egg
2–4 sausages

Mash the potato thoroughly with the flour and margarine.
Separate the egg yolk from the white and add half the yolk
to the potato mixture. Mix well together. Divide into three or
four portions and press each portion into a square. Easy with
floured hands! Fry the sausages lightly, place one on each
potato square and fold over to form a potato sausage roll.
Put on a greased baking dish, brush with a little beaten egg
white and bake at 350°F/Gas Mark 4 until lightly browned.

Note
Very tasty served with thick gravy.

Pork and Cheese Rissoles

1 egg
$\frac{1}{2}$ lb pork mince
$\frac{1}{2}$ small onion, finely chopped
$\frac{1}{4}$ eating apple, grated
Pinch of dried sage
Salt and pepper
3 small cubes cheese
Cooking oil

Separate the egg and add half the yolk to the pork. Mix
together with the onion, apple and sage. Season with salt
and pepper. With wet hands form the mixture into three
rounds and chill, if possible, for $\frac{1}{2}$ hour. Press a cube of cheese
firmly into the side of each rissole. Shallow fry in the oil until
golden brown, crisp and cooked through. Serve hot with
potatoes and broccoli or cauliflower.

Note
These are very tasty cold — serve with a mixed salad.

Sausage Schnitzels

2 pork sausages or 3 oz sausagemeat
Flour
1 egg, lightly beaten
1 tablespoon breadcrumbs
Cooking oil

Skin each sausage, put between foil or oiled greaseproof paper and flatten, or shape the sausagemeat into rounds. Dip in flour, then in lightly beaten egg and lastly in breadcrumbs. Chill if possible for 30 minutes. Fry on both sides in the hot oil until golden. Serve decorated with criss-cross strips of cheese and gherkin.

Grilled Pork Belly with Walnuts

2–3 slices pork belly
3 walnuts, chopped
½ cooking apple, chopped
½ teaspoon made mustard
Pinch of cayenne pepper
Salt

Grill the pork slices until brown and tender. Mix together the walnuts, apple, mustard and seasonings. Spread on the cooked pork and grill for a further 3 minutes.

Pork Stroganoff

4 oz pork fillet, cut into strips
Seasoned flour
½ oz butter
2 oz mushrooms, sliced
4 tablespoons natural yogurt

Toss the pork in seasoned flour in a paper bag. Heat the butter in a frying pan and fry the pork until lightly browned all over, turning frequently. Remove from the pan and keep warm. Add the mushrooms to the pan and cook until tender. Replace the pork in the pan, stir well and add the yogurt. Bring to the boil, check the seasoning, reduce the heat and simmer for about 20 minutes, stirring occasionally. Serve with boiled rice.

Hot Tongue

3–4 fresh lamb's tongues
1 pint stock (use water and a stock cube)
Bacon rinds
Salt and pepper
1 bay leaf
1 bouquet garni (optional)

Soak the tongues in cold salted water for 2 hours. Rinse well. Place in a pan and pour over sufficient hot stock to cover. Add the bacon rinds, salt, pepper and bay leaf. (If you have a packet of bouquet garni, then put one in.) Cover the pan and simmer over a low heat for 1–1½ hours. Peel off the skin while still hot and remove any gristle. Serve two hot tongues cut in slices. The stock can be thickened with a little corn-flour and served as gravy.

Note
It's worth cooking extra tongues as they can be pressed and eaten cold the next day or reheated with mushroom or sweet and sour sauce.

Tongue with Mild Mustard Sauce

A mild mustard sauce is delicious with hot tongue and is quick and easy to make. Place ½ oz margarine in a pan with ½ oz flour and ¼ pint milk and bring to the boil, whisking or stirring all the time. Stir in 1–2 teaspoons made mustard, blending well, and serve. (This sauce is equally good with ham and gammon.)

Tongue with Sweet and Sour Sauce

3–4 lamb's tongues

Sauce
1 level tablespoon cornflour
¼ pint cider
2 level tablespoons brown sugar
1 tablespoon cranberry sauce
1 tablespoon soy sauce
2 tablespoons vinegar

Soak the tongues in cold salted water for 2 hours and then cook them as directed in recipe for Hot Tongue (p. 125). When cooked, remove the skin and gristle and cut the tongues in half lengthwise. Replace them in the stock to reheat. Serve with the sweet and sour sauce and noodles.

To prepare the sauce: Blend the cornflour with a little of the cider. Pour into a saucepan. Add the remaining cider, brown sugar, cranberry sauce and soy sauce. Bring slowly to the boil, stirring continually, and then simmer for 5–10 minutes. Add the vinegar.

Tongue with Mushroom Sauce

2 cooked lamb's tongues
½ can condensed mushroom soup

Slice the skinned tongues and place in an ovenproof dish. Put ½ can condensed mushroom soup in a pan and heat gently. Pour over the tongue and cook at 350°F/Gas Mark 4 for 30 minutes. Serve with rice and peas.

Cold Tongue

To press tongue: Put two skinned tongues in a small bowl, cup or basin. Place the tongues in opposite directions and curl them round so that they fit tightly. Cover with a saucer, piece of foil or any greased paper and put a heavy weight on top. Leave overnight in a cool place.

6 Fish

Almost every sort of fish can be successfully fried, grilled, baked or poached. Fish is a versatile alternative to meat, and as white fish is low in calories it's a boon to dieters. A lot of people who are otherwise fond of fish are reluctant to cook it because they don't like to be left with a 'fishy' smell, so I've included lots of 'no-smell' recipes, including two for kippers. There are several ideas for using left-over cooked fish – but remember that cooked fish should be used within 24 hours.

Baked Fish with Cheese Crumble

1 cod or haddock steak
Salt and pepper
Lemon juice
½ oz margarine
1 heaped tablespoon flour
2 teaspoons grated cheese

Season the fish with salt and pepper and a sprinkling of lemon juice and place in a small, greased, ovenproof dish. Rub the margarine into the flour until it looks like fine breadcrumbs. Add the cheese and mix thoroughly. Sprinkle over the fish and bake at 350°F/Gas Mark 4 for 20–30 minutes until the fish is cooked and the top golden brown.

Haddock with Orange

1 haddock cutlet
Salt and pepper
Grated rind and juice of 1 small orange
1 teaspoon grated onion
2 teaspoons grated cheese
2 teaspoons brown breadcrumbs
½ oz margarine

Place the haddock cutlet in a small greased ovenproof dish. Season with salt and pepper and pour over the orange juice. Sprinkle on the grated orange rind and the grated onion. Top with the cheese and breadcrumbs. Dot with the margarine and bake at 350°F/Gas Mark 4 for 30–40 minutes.

Cod and Bacon Grill

1 cod steak
Margarine
Salt and pepper
1 bacon rasher
1 oz grated cheese

Brush the cod steak with melted margarine and season with salt and pepper. Grill gently with the bacon rasher for 5–8 minutes, then sprinkle the grated cheese over the fish. Continue grilling until the cheese has melted and browned. Serve the fish on a warm plate topped with the bacon rasher.

Note
You could grill a tomato at the same time: sprinkle a few toast crumbs on each tomato half and put a tiny piece of margarine on top before grilling.

Cod and Mushroom Bake

1 cod steak or fillet
½ can condensed cream of mushroom soup
1 tablespoon finely chopped onion (optional)
1 tablespoon milk

Place the cod steak in a small, lightly greased, ovenproof dish. Put the soup, milk and chopped onion into a bowl and stir well to remove any lumps. Pour over the fish and bake at 375°F/Gas Mark 5 for 25–30 minutes. Decorate with a sliced tomato and serve with toast triangles.

Notes
Haddock would be equally nice.
Some grated cheese could be sprinkled on top before the fish is cooked.

Baked Cod in Tomato Sauce

1 small can tomatoes
½ small onion
½ teaspoon dried mixed herbs
Salt
Black pepper
1 cod cutlet
½ oz soft margarine

Put the tomatoes and onion in a shallow ovenproof dish and sprinkle with the herbs, salt and black pepper. Place the fish on top. Dot the fish with the margarine and bake for 30 minutes at 375°F/Gas Mark 5.

Fish – Italian Style

1 small packet frozen broccoli
Salt and pepper
Knob of butter or margarine
1 cod or haddock steak or a fish fillet
¼ pint hot cheese sauce
1 tablespoon grated cheese
1 tablespoon fresh breadcrumbs

Cook the broccoli, drain well and season with salt and pepper. Place in a shallow, well-buttered fireproof dish. Poach or grill the fish and place on broccoli. Pour over the cheese sauce, mix the grated cheese and breadcrumbs and sprinkle on top. Grill for 5 minutes.

Notes
A squeeze of lemon juice and a little grated rind add extra flavour to the dish.
   Frozen spinach can be used instead of broccoli.

Fish Baked in Batter

2 oz flour
¼ pint milk
1 small egg
2 teaspoons water
½ oz butter or margarine
4–6 oz skinned smoked fish, cooked or raw

Beat together the flour, milk and egg with 2 teaspoons water. Grease a small baking dish thickly with the butter or margarine. Flake or chop the fish, put it in the dish and pour over the batter. Bake for 25–30 minutes at 325°F/Gas Mark 3. One or two quartered tomatoes can be added to the batter.

Grilled Fish with Crusty Cheese Topping

1–2 fish fillets
½ oz butter or soft margarine
Mayonnaise
2 oz grated cheese

Spread the fish fillets with a little butter or soft margarine and grill for 7–10 minutes, turning once. Spread mayonnaise on top and then add a thick layer of grated cheese. Grill for another 3 minutes until the cheese has set into a crusty layer.

Crispy Salmon Pie

½ can (10½-oz size) condensed cream of mushroom soup
3 tablespoons water
1 small (3½-oz) can pink salmon
2 oz cooked peas
1 teaspoon lemon juice
Pepper
Potato crisps

Heat the soup with the water in a small pan. Flake the salmon into small pieces and add to the soup with the peas and lemon juice. Season lightly with pepper. Turn into a small casserole or ovenproof dish. Cover the top with potato crisps and bake at 350°F/Gas Mark 4 for 15 minutes. Serve with extra potato crisps and a green vegetable.

Creamed Salmon and Peas

2 oz rice
Pinch of curry powder or turmeric (optional)
1 small (3½-oz) can salmon
1 small (5-oz) can processed peas
½ oz margarine
1 level tablespoon plain flour
6 tablespoons milk
Salt and pepper

Cook the rice in boiling, salted water for 12 minutes. Drain and stir in the curry powder or turmeric, if using, and keep warm. While the rice is cooking, drain the salmon, reserving the liquor. Remove the skin and flake the fish. Melt the margarine in a small saucepan, stir in the flour and cook for 2 minutes. Add the salmon liquor and milk. Bring to the boil, stirring. Cook for 2 minutes. Stir in the salmon and drained peas. Season with salt and pepper. Arrange the rice round the edge of a warm plate. Pour the salmon mixture in the centre and serve immediately.

Herring in Oatmeal

1 herring
Salt and pepper
2 tablespoons porridge oats or coarse oatmeal
Lard or butter

The herring can be filleted or left whole. Season with salt and pepper and dip in the oats. Press the oats on well. Fry the herring on both sides in hot lard or butter, allowing 2–3 minutes each side if filleted or 4–5 minutes each side if left whole.

Simple Soused Herring (or Mackerel)

1–2 fresh herrings or mackerel, filleted
1 level tablespoon finely chopped onion
1 bay leaf
6 peppercorns
Vinegar

Wash and dry the herring or mackerel pieces. Put some chopped onion on each piece and roll up. Place in a baking dish or casserole with the bay leaf and peppercorns, and pour over sufficient water and vinegar, in equal quantities, just to cover the fish. Cover the dish and cook in a slow oven 300°F/Gas Mark 2 for 1 hour.

Notes

Delicious hot or cold. If eating cold, always allow to cool in the liquid. Serve with boiled potatoes or potato salad.

If you're near a Sainsbury, you'll find they sell packets of fresh boned herrings.

Sugar Soused Herring

1–2 fresh herrings, filleted, or a packet of Sainsbury fresh
    boned herrings
½ onion, sliced
6 peppercorns
1 bay leaf
6 tablespoons cider
6 tablespoons vinegar
1 teaspoon brown sugar
½ carton sour cream for the sauce (optional)

Put the herrings in an ovenproof dish and place the onion slices on top. Mix the cider, vinegar and brown sugar and pour over the herrings. Add the peppercorns and bay leaf. Bake at 300°F/Gas Mark 2 for 1 hour. Remove from oven and leave to cool in liquid for 2 hours. Blend 1 tablespoon of fish liquid with ½ carton sour cream to make a sauce. Drain the herrings, place on a dish and pour over the sauce.

Very good with a cucumber salad.

Herring with Cider and Apple

2 small herrings
¼ pint cider
1 small red apple, skinned
½ carton plain yogurt

Split and bone the herrings and remove the heads. Place in an ovenproof dish. Pour over the cider and cook for 1 hour at 300°F/Gas Mark 2. Remove from oven and leave to cool in the liquid. Core the apple and cut into small cubes. Stir the apple pieces into the yogurt. Drain the herrings, place on a dish and pour over the apple and yogurt dressing.

Stuffed Herring with Apple and Onion Filling

1 herring

Filling
1 tablespoon onion, chopped
½ cooking apple, peeled, cored and diced
½ oz butter
¼ level teaspoon dried thyme
2 dessertspoons breadcrumbs

Split the herring and remove head and centre bone. Fill with prepared stuffing. Place in a buttered fireproof dish and dot with butter or wrap in buttered foil. Bake in a moderate oven 350°F/Gas Mark 4 for about 20–25 minutes.

To prepare the filling: Melt the butter in a pan and fry the onion until soft. Add the apple, cook for a couple of minutes. Stir in the thyme, breadcrumbs and season with salt and pepper. Mix well together.

Variation
BREAD AND ANCHOVY FILLING. The herring can also be stuffed with a mixture of 2 dessertspoons breadcrumbs and 2 finely chopped (or mashed) anchovy fillets or 1 teaspoon anchovy sauce. Season with lemon juice, black pepper and a pinch of dried basil.

Herring with Almonds

1 herring
8–10 blanched almonds or 1 tablespoon almond flakes
Pinch of dry mustard
1 heaped teaspoon plain flour
Salt
½ oz margarine
Parsley (optional)

Leave the herring whole but cut off the head. Score the skin in three places on each side with the point of a sharp knife. Mix the mustard, flour and a little salt together on a plate and dip the herring in this seasoned flour to coat. Melt the margarine in a frying pan, add the herring and fry for about 10 minutes, turning once. Remove from the pan and place on a warm plate. Add the almonds to the fat in the pan and fry quickly until golden brown – about 1 minute. Pour over the herring.

Kippers

To cook without any smell: Put the kipper in a jug or shallow dish and cover completely with boiling water. Cover the jug or dish with a plate or foil and leave for 5 minutes. They will be perfectly cooked and there will be no smell.

Kipper Kedgeree

2 oz long-grain rice
1 oz margarine or butter
1 kipper – whole or fillets
1 hard-boiled egg

Cook the rice in salted, rapidly boiling water for 12 minutes and drain. Melt the margarine or butter in a pan and stir in the rice. When heated through, add the skinned and chopped raw kipper and stir gently together for a few minutes until the mixture is hot. Mix in the hard-boiled egg and serve.

Note
A generous squeeze of lemon or a pinch of curry powder adds to the flavour.

To use cook-in-the-bag kippers for the Kedgeree
Cook the kippers according to the directions. Discard the skin and bones. Flake the flesh. Melt the butter in a pan. Stir in the rice with light movements. When heated through,

add the flaked fish and the hard-boiled egg and continue to heat, stirring gently, for a few minutes until really hot.

Quick Fish Pie

4–6 oz fish fillet
½ pint hot cheese sauce
1 hard-boiled egg, chopped
2–3 tablespoons peas
3 tablespoons grated cheese
3 tablespoons breadcrumbs
½ oz soft margarine

Cut the fish into ½-inch fingers, removing any skin and bones. Make up the cheese sauce, add the fish to the hot sauce and poach over a low heat for 5 minutes. Put a layer of chopped egg and peas in the bottom of a small baking or fireproof dish and pour over the fish and sauce. Cover with the grated cheese mixed with the breadcrumbs, dot with small knobs of soft margarine and brown under a low grill.

Variations
1. Crushed cornflakes can be used as a topping instead of breadcrumbs.
2. A pinch of curry powder or paprika, a little grated onion or some chopped parsley can be added to the seasoning.
3. Mashed potato can be spread over the fish. Season with pepper and sprinkle grated cheese on top before heating through.
4. Vary the pie with sliced mushrooms and canned chopped tomatoes.

Whiting with Cheese Meringue

1 small whole whiting
1 teaspoon tartare sauce
Whites of 2 small eggs
¼ teaspoon dried sage
¼ teaspoon mustard powder
2 tablespoons finely grated cheese, preferably Parmesan

Clean and trim the fish, leaving it whole, and place it in a greased ovenproof dish. Spread the tartare sauce on top. Whisk the egg whites until stiff, add the sage and mustard and whisk again. Fold in the grated cheese and spread the meringue mixture over the top of the fish. Sprinkle a little extra grated cheese on top and bake at 375°F/Gas Mark 5 for 20–25 minutes until golden.

Fish Ribbons

½–¾ lb whiting, plaice or lemon sole fillet
1 tablespoon seasoned flour
1 medium egg, lightly beaten
2 oz dried breadcrumbs
Oil or fat for deep frying
Salt

Cut the fish into strips, 1 inch wide and 2 inches long, with a sharp knife. Toss the fish pieces in the flour, dip in the egg and coat with the breadcrumbs. Deep fat fry the pieces for about 5 minutes. Drain well and sprinkle with salt. Serve with tomato or tartare sauce.

Notes
There is no need to deep fry in a *large* frying pan – you can manage very successfully with any small thick-bottomed saucepan. See the notes on Frying Temperatures (p. 45) to judge the right heat. After deep frying, leave the oil to cool down and, when quite cold, strain through a sieve into a screw-top jar. Leave in a cool place, ready to use again.
    Never strain hot oil.

Baked Lemon Sole

1 oz soft butter
1 medium-sized lemon sole
Salt and pepper
1 tablespoon lemon juice

Spread the butter liberally over a piece of foil, large enough to enclose the fish in a 'parcel'. Lay the fish in the centre, season with salt and pepper and sprinkle lemon juice over it. Fold up the foil around the fish and seal the edges firmly to form a loose 'parcel'. Place on a baking tray and bake in a moderately hot oven – 375°F/Gas Mark 5 – for about 25 minutes.

Note
Grilled lemon sole is very good too – brush with melted butter or soft margarine and season with salt, pepper and lemon juice. Grill under a medium heat, turning once, 10–12 minutes in all.

Devilled Mackerel

1 mackerel, cleaned and filleted
2 teaspoons breadcrumbs
1 teaspoon grated onion
Pinch of cayenne pepper
Pinch of mustard powder
1 tablespoon flour
1 oz butter

Mix together the breadcrumbs, onion, cayenne pepper and mustard. Spread the fillets with the stuffing and roll up. Secure with a cocktail stick or cotton. Roll in the flour and fry in the hot butter for approximately 5 minutes on each side.

Mackerel and Gooseberries

2 oz gooseberries
2 tablespoons water
1 mackerel, split and boned
Sugar, to taste
Salt and pepper
Butter

Simmer the gooseberries in the water, mashing them with a spoon while they cook until you have a thick purée. Season with salt, pepper and sugar. Open the fish out flat, spread the purée on one side and press the fish together again. Place in a buttered dish, cover with a greased paper and bake at 350°F/Gas Mark 4 for 30–40 minutes, according to the size of the fish.

Note
The stuffed mackerel can also be wrapped in a foil parcel.

Smoked Haddock with Poached Eggs

Poach the smoked haddock in a little milk, or milk and water mixed, over a low heat for 10–15 minutes. Drain carefully and top with a knob of butter or margarine and two poached eggs.

To poach eggs: Boil about 1 inch of water in a frying pan or small shallow pan and then lower the heat so that the water just simmers. Break an egg into a cup and transfer it gently into the water. If you drop it straight in, the white will spread badly. Cook gently, holding a spoon against one side of the egg to stop the white spreading; this takes about 3 minutes. Remove carefully – use a fish slice, if you have one.

Smoked Haddock Kedgeree

1 piece poached smoked haddock
2 oz long-grain rice
Margarine or butter
1 hard-boiled egg, chopped

Skin and bone the haddock and flake into small pieces. Cook
the rice in salted, rapidly boiling water for 12 minutes and
drain. Melt a nut of margarine or butter in a pan, add the
rice and haddock and heat slowly but thoroughly, stirring
gently. Add more margarine or butter if necessary. Mix in
the chopped hard-boiled egg and serve. If you have 1–2
tablespoons cream available, stir in at the end.

Notes
Kedgeree can also be made using a small (3½-oz) can of
salmon or tuna. Make up a packet of white sauce mix using
half the quantity of milk. Add a sliced hard-boiled egg, the
salmon or tuna and cooked rice.

If you have poached eggs on haddock one day, cook extra
fish to make kedgeree the next day. Skin and flake the extra
fish while it is still warm and leave covered in a cool place
overnight.

Scrambled Egg Smokie

3–4 oz *cooked* smoked cod, haddock or whiting fillet
2 eggs
1 tablespoon milk
Salt and pepper
½ oz butter or margarine

Flake the fish into small pieces. Beat the eggs with the milk
and stir in the fish. Season with salt and pepper and scramble
with the butter or margarine in the usual way. Serve with
brown bread and a tomato salad.

Note
This is a tasty way of using any smoked fish leftovers – so if you serve Smoked Haddock with Eggs one day, cook a little extra to make Scrambled Egg Smokie next day.

Fish with Celery

2–3 fish fillets
1 can celery hearts
¼ pint hot cheese sauce
Extra grated cheese

Roll the fish around the drained celery hearts and pack closely together in a small baking dish. Pour over 2 tablespoons of the celery liquid and cook at 350°F/Gas Mark 4 for 20 minutes. Pour over the hot cheese sauce, sprinkle extra grated cheese on top and brown under the grill.

Note
Extra celery hearts can be used as a vegetable tomorrow.

Salmon

Should you decide one day to treat yourself to a salmon steak, fresh or frozen, cook it either of the following ways and with hot, buttery new potatoes and peas you'll have a super meal.

Grilled Salmon

Season the salmon steak with salt and pepper and dust very lightly with flour. Melt a generous knob of butter in the bottom of the grill pan and turn the salmon over in it. Grill the fish for 8–10 minutes under a moderate heat, without turning. Baste occasionally with the juices. The fish is ready when it shrinks very slightly from the bone.

Baked Salmon

Butter a large piece of foil and place the salmon in the middle. Season lightly with salt and pepper. Fold up the edges of the foil to form a parcel, twisting the edges well together so that no juice can escape. Place the parcel on a baking dish or Pyrex plate and bake at 300°F/Gas Mark 2 for 20 minutes. If you are serving the fish cold, leave it to cool in the parcel.

Mussels

If you are lucky enough to buy fresh mussels they make a luxurious but quite a cheap treat. Buy yourself a quart of mussels for a main meal or a pint if you only want a snack.

To prepare: Throw away any open or broken mussels. Scrape and brush the mussels, remove the beards and leave them in a bowl under slowly running cold water for 30 minutes – this removes the sand and grit.

To cook: Put $\frac{1}{4}$ pint cheap dry white wine, dry cider or plain water into a large pan with a small sliced onion, $\frac{1}{2}$ bay leaf, 1 teaspoon chopped parsley and 1 oz butter. Add ground black pepper or a few peppercorns. Bring to the boil, add the mussels, cover well and leave over a brisk heat for 5–6 minutes, shaking the pan occasionally. The mussels should then be wide open and ready to eat – if they are still closed, allow another couple of minutes, but then discard any un-opened ones. Put the mussels into a soup bowl and pour over the cooking liquor. Mop up these delicious juices with crusty bread. If you can manage dry white wine or cider rather than water, it really does add a lot of extra flavour.

Soft Herring Roes

½ lb soft herring roes, large whole ones
1 egg, beaten
2–3 tablespoons dried breadcrumbs
Cooking oil for deep frying

Separate the roes and dry them a little. Dip in the beaten egg and coat with breadcrumbs. Deep fry in the hot oil until brown and crisp. Drain, sprinkle with salt and serve with tomato sauce and hot toast.

Note
Another way of cooking these roes is to toss them in a little seasoned flour and fry them in 1–2 oz hot, foaming butter.

7 Vegetables and Salads

VEGETABLES

These recipes aim to use vegetables as main meals. Mixed with cheese or another protein, vegetables make an interesting and cheap alternative to meat. Take advantage of seasonal vegetables – don't waste money on vegetables out of season, as you'll obviously be paying well over the odds. Think a little when you buy your vegetables – raw cauliflower or carrot in a salad one evening can be cauliflower cheese or hot buttered carrots the next.

Baked Stuffed Onion

1 large onion
2 slices ham, bacon or ham roll, finely chopped
1–2 tablespoons grated cheese
1 tablespoon fresh breadcrumbs
Pinch of dried sage
Salt and pepper
Knob of butter or margarine
Dripping or bacon fat
1 slice of bread

Peel and trim a shapely Spanish onion and cook in boiling salted water for 15–20 minutes until the outside is soft. Drain well and scoop out the centre with a spoon or sharp knife. Chop up the scooped out onion and mix it with the chopped meat, breadcrumbs, cheese and sage. Season with salt and pepper and stuff the onion centre with the mixture. Top with a knob of butter or margarine. Heat a little dripping or bacon fat in an ovenproof dish. Place the onion in the dish on a slice of buttered bread, cover and bake at 350°F/Gas Mark 4 for ¾–1 hour, basting frequently.

A little extra grated cheese can be sprinkled on top 20 minutes before the end of cooking and the dish should then be left uncovered.

Variations
The fillings can be varied by mixing the chopped onion centre with:

1. Minced or finely chopped cooked meat, chicken and sausage, or thinly sliced *raw* liver and kidney or smoked fish, a little fat, breadcrumbs and a pinch of mixed herbs.
2. Chopped tomatoes, breadcrumbs and cheese.
3. Bacon, grated cheese and breadcrumbs.
4. Chopped mushrooms, bacon and any thick sauce made with milk.

Stuffed Cabbage Leaves

Cook 6 large cabbage leaves in boiling water for 5 minutes. Drain and cut out any hard stalks. Put a spoonful of stuffing on to each leaf, roll up as neatly as possible and place in a casserole or ovenproof dish. Barely cover with ¼ pint stock (use water and ½ stock cube). Bring slowly to the boil and add a bay leaf, if handy. Cover and simmer gently for 1 hour on the stove or in the oven. The stock can be thickened with a little cornflour and water. Remove the cabbage rolls first to a hot plate.

Fillings

RICE AND BEEF. Mix together ¼ lb minced beef, 2 teaspoons finely chopped onion (or 1 teaspoon dried onion), 1 tablespoon water, 1 tablespoon cooked rice and 1 teaspoon tomato purée or ketchup. Season with salt and pepper.

SAUSAGEMEAT. Mix ¼ lb sausagemeat with 1 tablespoon cooked rice and a few drops of Worcester sauce or 1 teaspoon tomato ketchup.

Stuffed Marrow

½ small marrow
½ oz margarine
4 oz sausagemeat
1 small onion, finely chopped
2 oz mushrooms, sliced
Generous pinch of dried mixed herbs
Salt and pepper

Peel the marrow, cut into thick rings, remove seeds and cook for 10 minutes in boiling, salted water. Drain well and place in an ovenproof dish. Heat the margarine in a pan and fry the sausagemeat, onion and mushrooms for several minutes; drain and add the herbs. Season with salt and pepper. Put some of the filling in the centre of each marrow round. Place 3 tablespoons water in the dish, cover and cook at 350°F/Gas Mark 4 for 30–40 minutes.

Notes

Extra marrow can be used the following day. Cook the marrow, mash with margarine or butter and serve with cheese sauce and a poached egg.

Marrow can also be cut into small cubes and fried in a little margarine or dripping until golden brown. Sprinkle with salt and pepper before eating.

Stuffed Aubergine

1 medium–large aubergine
½ small onion, chopped
Cooking fat or oil
4 oz raw minced beef or any leftover cooked meat, finely chopped
2 tomatoes, skinned and roughly chopped
2 tablespoons breadcrumbs
Salt and pepper
¼ pint beef stock (use water and ½ stock cube)

Slice a 'lid' off the aubergine, scoop out the flesh and roughly chop. Sprinkle the inside of the shell with salt and leave upside down while preparing the filling. Cook the chopped onion in a little cooking fat or oil until soft. Add the minced beef and brown thoroughly. Stir in the chopped tomatoes, breadcrumbs, and chopped aubergine, and season with salt and pepper. Dry the aubergine shell with kitchen paper and spoon in the meat mixture. Replace the 'lid', put in a small ovenproof dish, pour round the stock, cover with a lid or piece of foil and bake at 350°F/Gas Mark 4 for 1 hour.

Stuffed Peppers

Cut the top off a large green or red pepper and scoop out the seeds and pith. Cook the pepper in boiling water for 3 minutes and then drain. When cool, brush the outside with oil or fat, fill, sprinkle the top with crumbs, dot with margarine and put in an ovenproof dish. Cover with a lid or kitchen foil and bake at 350°F/Gas Mark 4 for 30–40 minutes.

Fillings

1. Mixed cooked (left-over) vegetables moistened with tomato or cheese sauce.
2. Minced meat or sausagemeat mixed with breadcrumbs, grated onion and gravy. The meat can be browned first in a little fat.
3. Cooked rice mixed with chopped mushrooms and tomato.
4. A small can of baked beans mixed with grated cheese and a chopped fried bacon rasher.
5. 2 tablespoons parsley and thyme stuffing mixed with chopped mushrooms and corned beef and bound with a small egg.

Baked Potatoes

Wash a large potato, prick all over with a fork, rub a little salt into the skin (to make it crisp and tasty) and bake for $1-1\frac{1}{2}$ hours at 375°F/Gas Mark 5. *Or*, to save cooking time, cut the potato in half, wipe dry the cut side and place cut side down on a greased tin. Cook at 375°F/Gas Mark 5 for 30–40 minutes.

When cooked, slit open, add a knob of butter or margarine and/or any of the toppings listed below.

Toppings

1. Grated Cheese.
2. Crisply fried bacon – a little bacon fat poured on the potato first is delicious.

3. Mashed hard-boiled egg with chutney and salad cream.
4. Baked beans.
5. Mashed pilchard in tomato sauce.
6. Cottage cheese.
7. Poached, fried or scrambled eggs.
8. Fried sausages.
9. Chopped fried kidneys.

Note

If you have any sausagemeat handy, remove the centre of a large potato, using an apple corer, and fill with the sausagemeat, wrap in a bacon rasher, cover with foil and bake at 400°F/Gas Mark 6 for 1 hour.

Cauliflower Cheese

The quickest way to make cauliflower cheese is to cut up and cook half a cauliflower in boiling water and, while it is cooking, make up half a packet of cheese sauce mix. Drain the cauliflower, pour on the cheese sauce, sprinkle a little grated cheese on top and brown under a low grill.

Variations

1. A plain white sauce mix can be used – just add 2 tablespoons grated cheese when it is made and stir until all the cheese has melted.
2. Lightly butter 1–2 slices of hot toast, spread with mustard and place the cauliflower on top. Then add the sauce and cheese.

Leek, Bacon and Potato Pie

1–2 bacon rashers, derinded and cut in cubes
Cooking fat
2 leeks
2 tablespoons stock or water

1 small egg
1 teaspoon creamy milk or cream
Mashed potato

Cook the bacon cubes in a little fat until they are just begin-
ning to brown. Add the washed and sliced white part of the
leeks and cook gently for 5 minutes. Pour on the stock, or
water, and cook over a low heat for 10–15 minutes. Turn into
a shallow ovenproof dish, season and add the egg beaten up
with the milk or cream. Cover with mashed potato and bake
at 400°F/Gas Mark 6 for 15 minutes.

Note
Chopped cooked ham can be used instead of the bacon – add
it to the leeks with the stock.

Mixed Vegetable Pie

½ pint cheese sauce
6–8 oz assorted cooked vegetables, diced
2 tablespoons peas
2 oz cooked macaroni
2 tablespoons grated cheese
2 tablespoons breadcrumbs

Make up the cheese sauce, stir in the macaroni, peas and
assorted vegetables and allow to heat through. Turn into a
baking dish. Sprinkle with cheese and breadcrumbs and grill
for 5–10 minutes.

Note
A chopped hard-boiled egg, bacon, cooked meat or sausage
can be added to the pie.

Cabbage Hot Pot

¼ cabbage, shredded
½ onion, peeled and sliced
¼ pint stock (use water and ½ stock cube)
2 oz ham or bacon
Cooking fat
Salt and pepper
Mustard

Heat a little fat in a pan and fry the sliced onion until transparent. Add the stock and bring to the boil; then add the shredded cabbage and cook for 5 minutes. Chop the ham or bacon and add to the pan. Season to taste with salt, pepper and a little mustard.

Sweetcorn Pudding

1 small egg
2 tablespoons cream, or top of the milk
1 small can sweetcorn, drained
2 tablespoons breadcrumbs
1 tablespoon grated cheese
Salt and pepper

Beat the egg and cream or top of the milk, stir in the sweetcorn and breadcrumbs, and season with salt and pepper. Turn into a buttered dish. Sprinkle the cheese on top and bake at 350°F/Gas Mark 4 for 20–25 minutes.

Note
Good served with crisply fried bacon.

Potato Pancakes

2 medium-sized potatoes
1 dessertspoon self-raising flour
2 teaspoons finely grated onion (optional)
1 small egg

Cooking fat or dripping
Salt and pepper

Peel the potatoes, soak in cold water for 30 minutes, then grate and drain away any liquid. Add the flour, onion and beaten egg. Mix thoroughly and season with salt and pepper. Melt a little fat or dripping in a pan and drop in the mixture in spoonfuls. When brown on one side, turn over and brown the other side.

Globe Artichoke

This makes a very nice one-person treat.

First, cut the stalk level with the leaves. Soak the artichoke in cold salted water for an hour to remove any grit or dirt. Then put the artichoke in a saucepan, add a teaspoon of salt and cover with boiling water. Cook in steadily boiling water for 45 minutes to 1 hour, depending on size. If the water does not completely cover the artichoke, turn it over halfway through. To test if cooked, pull away one of the leaves; if it slips out easily, then the artichoke is ready. Leave it upside down on the draining board for a few minutes.

To eat: Pull away the leaves with your fingers and dip the fleshy ends into melted butter. When you reach the middle, cut off the thistly centre and then eat the most prized part, the base, with a knife and fork.

Avocado

The avocado has been included in this section although it really is a delicately flavoured fruit. It is often called a 'pear', but that is on account of its shape and, unlike the *real* pear, its skin is never eaten.

If you want to test an avocado's ripeness, *don't* pinch or squeeze it. Cradle it in the palm of your hand and if it yields to gentle all-over pressure, it is ready to eat. If you buy an unripe avocado, leave it to ripen in the fruit bowl or, if you want to speed up the ripening, wrap it in newspaper. *Never* use an unripe avocado.

However you serve it, always start by cutting it in half lengthways and carefully twisting the halves to separate them. Stick the sharp tip of the knife into the stone, twist the handle a little and, as long as the avocado is ripe, it is easy to lift out the stone. Brush the surface with a little lemon juice to avoid any discolouration and, if you are only using half, wrap the other half with the stone in it in foil or plastic food wrap and keep it in the refrigerator.

Simple Avocado Ideas

Halve the avocado and remove the stone.

Fill the centre with a little oil and vinegar dressing, or try filling the avocado with one of the following:

1. Cottage or cream cheese with chopped nuts.
2. Flaked cooked chicken with chopped tomato or pepper.
3. Flaked salmon or tuna with sweetcorn.
4. Chopped hard-boiled egg with cooked rice and peas.

Or try it sweet – lots of people prefer to eat the avocado with sugar, fruit or ice cream.

P.S. If you have green fingers don't throw the stone away; grow your own avocado plant indoors! Place the base of the stone in water – you can suspend it over a jam jar with the aid of a few toothpicks and leave it until it sprouts roots and shoots. Be patient, as it sometimes takes a month or so before anything happens! Then plant it in soil and it will grow into a small decorative tree.

SALADS

It's worth being a little adventurous when you're preparing a salad! The days of the limp lettuce leaf and sad tomato are gone. These eighteen salad ideas are a few suggestions to be going on with, so do experiment yourself with raw vegetables and fruit. Try using chopped avocado, cold boiled potatoes, butter beans or green beans with a French dressing. The most unlikely ingredients can make a tasty salad which is a nourishing and satisfying meal in itself. Don't forget that if you make a large quantity of salad dressing you can keep it for about a week in the 'fridge, stored in a glass container with a tight-fitting top.

Coleslaw

Finely shred some white cabbage and moisten with salad cream. To vary, add grated carrot, grated apple and finely chopped pineapple.

Apple, Carrot and Cauliflower

Mix grated raw cauliflower and carrot with chunks of eating apple. Moisten with salad cream.

Fruit and Cheese

Mix fresh or canned orange and/or grapefruit segments with cottage cheese. Serve on lettuce and sprinkle a few chopped nuts on top. *Or* pile cottage cheese into drained peach or pear halves.

Celery, Apple and Date

Mix sliced celery with grated apple and chopped dates.

Ham, Chicory and Cheese

Slice a small head of chicory and mix with some chopped ham and grated cheese. Toss in salad cream.

Macaroni Salad

Mix cooked macaroni with a small can of flaked tuna, a sliced hard-boiled egg, a few olives and tomato quarters, and dress with French dressing.

Raisin and Carrot

Mix grated carrot with raisins and moisten with salad cream or orange juice.

Banana Crunch

Mix one sliced banana with a sliced celery and chopped nuts. Sprinkle on lemon juice and moisten with salad cream. Serve on lettuce.

Chicory, Orange and Watercress

Wash a small head of chicory and separate the leaves. Mix with peeled, sliced orange and watercress.

Sausage and Beetroot

Mix one peeled cooked beetroot, cut in chunks, with 2–3 cooked sliced pork sausages or frankfurters and 3 chopped spring onions.

Sunny Peach Salad

Mix 2 sliced canned peaches with cold cooked rice, raisins, watercress and chopped ham.

Mushroom and Pepper

Slice 2 oz mushrooms (use an egg slicer for speed) and mix with a small thinly sliced green pepper and lots of finely chopped parsley.

Cucumber in Sour Cream

Thinly slice or dice a chunk of cucumber. Blend $\frac{1}{2}$ carton sour cream with a little salt, pepper and lemon juice, and toss the cucumber in this dressing. Add some chopped chives or parsley, or a sieved hard boiled egg yolk.

Italian Vegetable Salad

Mix 2 oz cooked rice with a small packet of cooked frozen mixed vegetables. Decorate with a few anchovy strips and a sliced hard-boiled egg.

Bean and Tomato

Mix a thickly sliced tomato with a small can of drained butter beans or cooked frozen French beans and a little finely chopped onion.

Courgette and Tomato

Plunge 2–3 courgettes (baby marrows) into boiling salted water. Simmer for 6–8 minutes, drain, cool and then slice. Mix with sliced tomato and chopped onion. Fry a few coarse fresh breadcrumbs – brown ones are nice – in a little butter or margarine. Mix with Parmesan cheese and scatter over the salad.

Crisp Cauliflower

Cook some cauliflower flowerets in boiling salted water for 2–3 minutes. Drain and leave to cool. Don't overcook. Mix with lettuce, sliced celery and cucumber.

Spinach, Mushroom and Bacon

My own favourite! Wash and pat dry some raw spinach leaves, tear into pieces and mix with thinly sliced raw mushrooms. Fry 1–2 bacon rashers until very crisp and crumble into the salad. Toss in a little French dressing.

SALAD DRESSINGS

French Dressing

Put 3 tablespoons olive or salad oil, 1 dessertspoon vinegar, a generous pinch of salt, pepper and dry mustard, and $\frac{1}{4}$ teaspoon sugar into a screw-top jar and shake until well blended. This dressing can be kept for at least a week in a cool larder or refrigerator – store the dressing in a covered jar or container.

Variations
1. Substitute lemon juice for the vinegar.
2. Add a very small clove of crushed garlic or a pinch of garlic salt.
3. Add $\frac{1}{2}$ teaspoon finely chopped mint and another $\frac{1}{2}$ teaspoon sugar.
4. Add finely chopped parsley.
5. Stir in $\frac{1}{2}$ finely chopped small hard-boiled egg and a little parsley.

Mock Mayonnaise

½ level teaspoon French or English made mustard
¼ teaspoon salt
Small pinch of white pepper
1 level teaspoon sugar
4 tablespoons evaporated milk
4 tablespoons olive oil
1–2 tablespoons wine vinegar

Put the mustard, salt, pepper and sugar in a bowl with the milk. Whisk or beat in the olive oil, little by little. Gradually add the vinegar – this will thicken up the dressing. This dressing will keep for up to 24 hours in a cool place.

Yogurt Dressing

Mix together ½ carton natural yogurt, 1 teaspoon lemon juice, salt and pepper and a little finely chopped parsley (or a few chopped chives).

8 Pastas, Eggs and Simple Snacks

PASTAS

COOKING METHOD

There are lots of different varieties of pasta and they all make a quick and tasty meal. If you've always eaten macaroni, then it's time to try a packet of spaghetti, vermicelli, tagliatelle noodles or 'shells'. Once opened, put the packet in a container with an airtight lid and keep in a dry place.

For a main meal you'll want 2–3 oz pasta and the best way to cook it is in lots of fast-boiling salted water, allowing 12–15 minutes for spaghetti and 15–20 minutes for macaroni, tagliatelle and shells. You can stop the pasta from sticking together, and to the pan, by adding a tcaspoon of cooking oil to the water; otherwise keep stirring the water round while it is cooking. Don't overcook it or it will be soft and mushy; it should be just a little bit firm – as the Italians say, *al dente*. Test to see if it's done by biting a piece. Once cooked, drain it well, tip it on to a warm plate and stir in a knob of butter or margarine. Eat it just as it is with lots of grated cheese sprinkled on top or pour over one of these sauces:

Fast Tomato Sauce

Empty a small can of tomatoes into a pan and heat with a little butter. Season with salt, pepper and a pinch of sugar.

Meat and Tomato Sauce (Bolognese)

1 small onion, chopped
4 oz minced beef
2 tablespoons cooking oil
1 small can tomatoes
2 teaspoons tomato purée
6 tablespoons stock (use water and $\frac{1}{4}$ stock cube)
Generous pinch of sugar
Generous pinch of dried mixed herbs
Salt and pepper

Cook the chopped onion in the oil until soft. Turn up the heat and fry the minced beef until brown. Add the tomatoes, tomato purée, a generous pinch of sugar, the stock and a generous pinch of dried mixed herbs. Season with salt and pepper and simmer for 30–45 minutes. If you like the taste of garlic, chop a small clove and cook it with the onions, or add a pinch of garlic salt.

Creamy Mushroom Sauce

½ oz butter or margarine
3 oz mushrooms, sliced
½ small onion, chopped
Salt and pepper
3 tablespoons sour cream (or plain yogurt and a squeeze of
     lemon juice)
Tomato ketchup or Worcester sauce

Melt the butter or margarine in a pan and add the sliced
mushrooms and the chopped onion. Cover and cook for
10 minutes. Season with salt and pepper. Remove from the
heat, stir in the sour cream (or plain yogurt and a squeeze of
lemon juice) and a few drops of tomato ketchup or Worcester
sauce and pour over the pasta.

Variation
You could add sliced mushrooms to ⅓ can condensed cream
of mushroom soup thinned with 3 tablespoons milk.

Chicken Liver Sauce

Make the Fast Tomato Sauce. Chop 2–3 chicken livers into
small pieces, cook quickly in a little hot butter until brown
and add with their juice to the tomato sauce. Stir together
and pour over the pasta. You can add a few sliced mushrooms
to this sauce or a chopped crisply fried bacon rasher.

Tomato, Bacon and Pepper Sauce

2–3 bacon rashers
1 small can of tomatoes
1 small green or red pepper, finely chopped

Derind the bacon rashers and cut into small squares. Heat
the bacon rinds in a pan and use the fat to fry the bacon
squares until nice and crisp. Add the tomatoes and the
chopped red or green pepper. Simmer for 20 minutes.

Notes
Spaghetti, noodles and macaroni can be cooked ahead. As soon as they are cooked, drain and run under cold water. Leave in a bowl, completely covered with cold water, until needed. Then drain well. Melt a little margarine in a pan and shake the pasta for a few minutes.

Noodles with Ham

2 oz cooked ham
3 oz tagliatelle or macaroni
1 oz butter or margarine
Grated cheese

Cut the cooked ham into strips. Cook the tagliatelle or macaroni, drain well and place on a hot plate. Add the butter or margarine to the pan and cook the ham strips for 2–3 minutes. Pour on to the pasta and sprinkle grated cheese on top.

Spaghetti Bake

1 medium onion, sliced
1 oz butter
Salt and pepper
Pinch of mixed herbs
3 oz long spaghetti
1 (14-oz) can tomatoes
Grated cheese, preferably strong Cheddar

Fry the sliced onion in the hot butter until golden brown. Place in an ovenproof dish and season with salt, pepper and herbs. Break the dry spaghetti into 3-inch lengths and scatter over the top of the onion; then pour the tomatoes over the spaghetti – it should be covered. Grate the cheese in an even layer over the top. Cover with kitchen foil or a lid and bake in a slow oven 300°F/Gas Mark 2 for 1½ hours. Remove the foil and raise the heat to 375°F/Gas Mark 5 for 10–15 minutes to brown.

GRILLED, TOASTED OR FRIED SNACKS

Bacon and Cheese

Toast a slice of bread on one side only. Place a slice of cheese spread with mustard on the untoasted side, cover with a bacon rasher and grill until the bacon is cooked.

Tomato Toasties

Place thick tomato slices on a round of hot buttered toast, cover with finely chopped onion and season with salt and pepper. Place a slice of cheese on top, then a bacon rasher and grill until the bacon is crisp. *Or* just cover with thick tomato slices, top with a paste made of breadcrumbs and salad cream, and grill for 5–10 minutes.

Ham and Banana Splits

Split a bread roll lengthwise, without cutting completely through it; butter the roll and spread with a little made mustard. Cut a banana in half and roll it in ham. Place this inside the bread roll, sprinkle thickly with grated cheese and grill.

Crumpets – Pizza Style

Toast and butter 1–2 crumpets. Sprinkle grated cheese on top. Add thin slices of tomato and then some more cheese. Arrange drained anchovy fillets in a criss-cross pattern on top. Cook under a medium grill until the cheese melts and turns golden brown. Can be decorated with black olives.

Mexican Toasted Cheese

2 oz grated cheese
1 tablespoon tomato purée
1 tablespoon breadcrumbs
¼ teaspoon made mustard
2 tablespoon sweetcorn
Pinch of cayenne (optional)

Put all the ingredients in a small pan and stir over a gentle heat until smooth and hot. Do not boil. Serve on rounds of hot buttered toast.

Cheese Fritters

Place a thin slice of cheese, seasoned with mustard, between 2 slices of day-old bread. Cut into quarters and press together. Fry in butter or oil until brown on both sides.

Ham Snack

Put a slice of bread on a fireproof dish and soak in a little beer. Cover with cheese, place a slice of ham on top and cover that with more cheese. Place under a hot grill until the cheese melts. Top with a fried egg.

Marmalade Muffins

Spread some split muffins or halved rolls with marmalade, top with a slice of cheese and grill.

Luncheon Meat Grill

2 rounds of bread
Butter
2 slices of luncheon meat
2 apple rings
1 tablespoon sultanas
1 tablespoon grated cheese

Fry the bread lightly or toast and butter it. Put a slice of meat on each piece and top with an apple ring, filling the centre with sultanas. Sprinkle with cheese and grill.

Six Quick Toast Toppings

To be served on hot buttered toast, toasted rolls or fried bread.

1. Cooked streaky bacon with fried banana.
2. Flaked canned salmon or tuna mixed with a little salad cream and seasoning to taste.
3. Grilled kipper fillets sprinkled with grated cheese and lemon juice.
4. Liver or meat paste topped with fried onion.
5. Sliced canned mushrooms topped with processed cheese and grilled until brown.
6. Sardines mashed with a little vinegar and topped with chopped celery.

SNACKS

Apple and Cheese Crumble

Breadcrumbs
2 eating apples, peeled, cored and sliced
3 oz grated crumbly cheese – Lancashire, Wensleydale
¼ pint milk
½ oz margarine or butter

Put a layer of breadcrumbs at the bottom of a small, lightly greased, baking dish. Add half the apple slices and then half the cheese. Repeat the layers. Pour on the milk and sprinkle breadcrumbs on top. Dot with the margarine or butter. Bake at 350°F/Gas Mark 4 for 30 minutes.

Pancakes

2 oz flour
1 small egg
¼ pint milk (or milk and water mixed)
1 teaspoon salad oil or melted margarine or butter

To prepare the pancake batter: Sift the flour with a pinch of salt into a bowl. Break the egg into the middle. Gradually stir in half the milk. Add the oil, margarine or butter and beat in the rest of the milk. Cover and leave to stand in a cool place for 30 minutes.

To make each pancake: Pour a tablespoon of the mixture into a hot, lightly greased, small frying pan. You need just enough batter to cover the bottom of the pan thinly. Cook for a minute and then toss or turn with a knife, spatula, or fish slice and cook the other side for a minute. Turn out on to a plate sprinkled with sugar and spread with jam or marmalade; or roll up and eat with fruit, honey, ice cream or cottage cheese.

Put any left-over pancakes in a polythene bag or container, with a piece of greaseproof paper between each pancake, and store in a refrigerator or cool larder. They will keep for several days and can be reheated on a plate over boiling water or in a low oven.

Toad in the Hole

Make up the pancake batter as in the previous recipe. Preheat the oven to 400°F/Gas Mark 6. Put a little dripping, oil or lard in a small baking tin and place in the oven. When the fat is hot, add 2–3 skinless sausages and return to the oven for 5 minutes. Pour on the batter and bake for another 30 minutes.

Coddled Egg in a Cup

Put a knob of butter or margarine in a strong teacup and stand the cup in a saucepan of simmering water – the water should come halfway up the cup. When the fat has melted, drop in an egg, put a lid or plate on the pan and cook over a low heat for 4 minutes. A little finely chopped ham and/or parsley can be put in the cup just before the egg. Serve on buttered toast.

Baked Bacon, Bread, Sausage and Tomato

Ideal for a large cooked breakfast – or brunch!

4 thin rashers streaky bacon
2 chipolata sausages
2 slices bread, without crusts
Butter or margarine
2 tomatoes

Remove rind from the bacon rashers and wrap 2 rashers round each sausage. Lightly butter the bread and place, buttered side down, on a baking sheet or in an ovenproof dish. Put the bacon-wrapped sausages diagonally on each piece of bread. Cut the tomatoes in half and place, cut side up, on the bread either side of the sausages. Bake for 25 minutes at 400°F/Gas Mark 6.

Grilled Grapefruit

Sprinkle half a grapefruit with a teaspoon of brown sugar and dot with a little butter. Place in grill pan and cook under a medium grill for 5–10 minutes until the top browns and the fruit is heated through. Eat hot.

Corn and Cheese Omelette

2 eggs
Salt and pepper
1 tablespoon water
½ oz butter
2–3 tablespoons sweetcorn
1 tablespoon grated cheese

Beat the eggs lightly with the water and season with salt and pepper. Heat the butter in a frying pan, tilting the pan to grease the whole surface. Pour in the egg mixture and immediately start stirring gently with the back of a fork, from the sides towards the centre, until no liquid egg remains. Stop stirring and cook a little longer to lightly brown the underneath. Spread the drained sweetcorn down the centre and towards one side. Sprinkle on the cheese. Tilt the pan and let the omelette fold over. Turn on to a warm plate.

Egg and Tomato Jumble

Melt a knob of butter in a small pan, add a sliced tomato and cook for 5 minutes. Add an egg beaten up with a tablespoon of grated cheese. Season with salt and pepper. Stir until thick. Serve on hot toast.

Variations
Instead of the tomato, you could use any chopped cooked left-over vegetables, cooked bacon or sausage pieces.

Tasty Supper Dish

2–3 slices bread and butter, without the crusts
1 eating apple, cored and sliced
2 tomatoes, sliced
1 stick celery, sliced
2 oz grated cheese

Butter a small pie dish and line with the bread and butter. Fill in the centre with the apple, tomato and celery and cover with the grated cheese. Bake at 375°F/Gas Mark 5 for 15–20 minutes – the outside of the bread should be crisp and light brown.

Spicy Eggs in a Rice Ring

2 oz long-grain rice
½ can mulligatawny soup
1 level tablespoon cornflour
1 heaped teaspoon tomato purée
1 level tablespoon sweet chutney
2 hard-boiled eggs, shelled and cut in half
1 tablespoon sultanas
½ oz margarine or butter

Cook the rice in fast-boiling salted water for 12–15 minutes. While the rice is cooking, pour the soup into a small pan, bring to the boil and thicken with the cornflour, mixed first with the little water. Stir in the tomato purée and chutney. Drain the rice, add a knob of margarine or butter and the sultanas, and fluff up with a fork. Arrange the rice around a plate, put the halved eggs in the centre and pour over the spicy sauce.

Cheese Relish

1 cup fresh white breadcrumbs
2 cups milk
1 egg
½ oz soft margarine
Salt and pepper
¼ cup grated cheese

Soak the breadcrumbs in the milk. Stir in the well-beaten egg, the margarine, salt and pepper and the grated cheese. Mix thoroughly and bake in a small greased oven dish at 350°F/Gas Mark 4 until brown and nicely set.

French Toast

Beat together 1 egg and ¼ cup milk. Put 2 slices of bread in the mixture and turn until both sides are well soaked. Melt a little butter in a large pan until bubbly. Add the soaked bread. After a couple of minutes, turn the bread and brown the other side. Meanwhile soak 2 more slices of bread in the egg/milk mixture. Remove the browned French Toast to a plate. Fry the other slices. Top with honey or jam, or serve with bacon or sausages.

Cinammon Toast

Mix 3 teaspoons castor sugar with 1 teaspoon ground cinammon and sprinkle over hot, buttered toast. Delicious at tea-time!

Swiss Egg

Toast a slice of bread on one side, cover the untoasted side with grated cheese and make a hollow in the centre. Place the yolk of an egg in the centre of the cheese. Season with salt and pepper. Whisk the egg white until stiff and cover the egg yolk and cheese. Cook at 400°F/Gas Mark 6 until golden brown.

Savoury Bacon

2 thick rashers collar bacon
1 egg, beaten
Sage and onion stuffing mix
Lard for frying

Derind the rashers and dip into the beaten egg. Toss in the dry sage and onion stuffing mixture, and fry in shallow lard until tender on the inside and crisp on the outside – approximately 6 minutes.

Hidden Eggs

Mashed potato (use instant)
1 small packet frozen chopped spinach
½ packet cheese sauce mix
¼ pint milk
2 eggs

Salt and pepper
Spread the mashed potato at bottom of a shallow ovenproof dish. Make up the cheese sauce with milk as directed on the packet. Cook the spinach, drain well and add to the warm sauce. Make two hollows in the potato and drop an egg into each. Carefully spoon the sauce over and cook for 10 minutes at 400°F/Gas Mark 6.

Note
This is a variation of Egg Florentine (poached eggs on hot spinach with a cheese sauce poured on top).

Cheese Soufflé

½ can (10½-oz size) condensed cream of celery soup
2 oz grated cheese
2 eggs

Mix the cheese and soup together in a pan and warm slowly until the cheese has melted. Remove from the heat. Separate the eggs and stir in the egg yolks. Whisk the egg whites until stiff and fold into the soup mixture. Pour into a greased 1-pint pudding basin and bake at 375°F/Gas Mark 5 for 30 minutes.

9 A Few Puddings

This chapter on puddings is deliberately rather short. There are so many ready-made desserts on the market today that it's really better to use your time and imagination on a well-planned main course. But if you are a pudding fanatic, then make the baked puddings when you are using the oven for your main course and save on oven time.

Bread and Butter Pudding

2–4 slices bread, without crusts – white, brown or currant
    loaf
Butter for spreading
1–2 level tablespoons mincemeat
1 standard egg
Milk
1–2 teaspoons brown sugar, preferably demerara

Butter the bread. Cut in pieces to fit a small ovenproof dish.
Put half the buttered bread on the bottom of the dish, butter
side down. Add a layer of mincemeat. Cover with the
remaining bread, butter side up. Beat the egg, make up to
¼ pint with milk and pour over the bread. Sprinkle sugar on
top. Bake for 20 minutes at 350°F/Gas Mark 4 until set and
golden crisp on the top. Serve with cream or custard.

Variations
1. Jam or marmalade can be used instead of mincemeat to
vary the flavour.
2. Try adding a layer of apple slices and finely chopped
dates, or a tablespoon of currants, raisins or sultanas.

Prune and Apricot Compôte

2 oz dried apricots
2 oz dried prunes
3–4 tablespoons strained cold tea
1 tablespoon raisins
2 tablespoons honey

Soak the dried fruits overnight in the cold tea and sufficient
water to cover the fruit by a depth of 1 inch. Drain the fruit.
Put the fruit and raisins into a saucepan and pour over the
honey, which has been dissolved in ¼ pint warm water.
Simmer for 20 minutes until plump and just tender; alternatively, bake the fruits in a casserole in a moderate oven.
Serve hot or cold with custard or cream.

Note
A thickly sliced banana can be added to the compôte.

Baked Apple

Core a large cooking apple, score the skin around the centre and fill with one of the following:

1. Chopped dates and honey.
2. Mincemeat.
3. Apricot jam and chopped preserved ginger.
4. Raisins and brown sugar.
5. Marmalade and chopped nuts.

Put a knob of butter on top. Place in a small ovenproof dish. Cover the bottom of the dish with water and a teaspoon of sugar. Bake at 375°F/Gas Mark 5 for 1 hour, basting occasionally with the syrup.

Variation
A variation of baked apple is to peel, core and slice the cooking apple. Arrange the slices in a small ovenproof dish or on a Pyrex plate. Sprinkle with sugar and raisins and put a few small knobs of butter on top. Cook, uncovered, at 300°F/Gas Mark 2 until soft and golden brown – 35–45 minutes. Delicious eaten warm with cream.

Zabaglione

Easier to make than to pronounce, this is a delicious one-person pudding.

2 egg yolks
2 teaspoons castor sugar
1–2 tablespoons Marsala wine or sweet sherry
Sponge fingers

Put the egg yolks, castor sugar and Marsala wine or sweet sherry in a thick basin. Place over a pan of hot water and whisk until thick and frothy and the consistency of lightly whipped cream. Turn into a glass and serve warm with sponge fingers.

Apple with a Toffee Top

Spoon thick, sweetened apple purée (fresh or canned) into a small fireproof dish. Top with a layer of soured cream and then cover with brown sugar. Place under a hot grill for a couple of minutes. The sugar will form a hard toffee crust, but be careful not to let it burn.

Simple Steamed Custard

Very soothing.

1 egg
2 dessertspoons sugar
1 cup hot milk
Grated nutmeg

Put the egg and sugar in a basin and stand the basin in a pan of hot water. Beat lightly with a fork and then add the milk and nutmeg. Cover the basin with a saucer – to prevent steam from spoiling the custard – and leave for 10 minutes. To test if the custard has set, remove the saucer and gently shake the basin.

Blackcurrant Custard

2 oz fresh blackcurrants
1 large egg
½ pint milk
1 level tablespoonful castor sugar
Drop of vanilla essence

Butter the inside of a small ovenproof dish. Wash the fruit, remove any stalks and place in the dish. Beat the egg, mix

MEMO

International
2520 and 2530
'Site Handlers'

Fork Lifts for Rough Site Work

Pearl barley.
neck or breast of lamb
onion
carrot
turnip.
leek
cheese
butter
bread.

in the milk, sugar and vanilla essence, and pour over the fruit. Bake for 45 minutes at 350°F/Gas Mark 4.

Sugary Peaches

Cream a little butter with the same amount of soft brown sugar and a squeeze of lemon juice. Fill hollows of drained canned peach halves and place under a medium grill for 2–3 minutes. Serve hot with a little cream.

Orange Dessert

Peel an orange and slice thinly. Sprinkle on a little lemon juice. Pour over chilled evaporated milk and sprinkle with grated chocolate.

Bananas in Orange Sauce

1 oz sugar
1 orange
3 tablespoons water
1 oz butter
1 tablespoon Cointreau or orange liqueur (optional)
1–2 bananas, peeled and halved lengthways

Put the sugar, grated rind of the orange and the water in a frying pan. Heat very gently until the sugar has dissolved. Bring to the boil and simmer for 5 minutes. Add the orange juice and butter and cook over a low heat until the butter has melted. Add the Cointreau or orange liqueur and the bananas. Cook for a further 5 minutes. Serve immediately. Nice with cream.

Tipsy Banana

1–2 bananas
A little sherry or rum
Brown sugar
Cream

Peel the bananas and prick all over with a fork. Place in an ovenproof dish and pour over the sherry or rum. Leave to soak in and then sprinkle generously with brown sugar. Bake at 350°F/Gas Mark 4 for 20–30 minutes. Serve hot with cream.

Fruit Crumbles

Put some stewed or drained canned fruit in a small greased ovenproof dish and sweeten if necessary. Apples, rhubarb, gooseberries and blackberries are particularly nice. If you want to use uncooked fruit, cut it into small pieces and put it uncovered into the oven in the ovenproof dish while you make the crumble topping so that it can start cooking.

Toppings

Rub 1 oz margarine or butter into 3 oz flour until it resembles fine breadcrumbs. Mix in 1 oz sugar and a pinch of ginger, cinammon or nutmeg. Sprinkle the crumble mixture on top of the fruit and bake at 350°F/Gas Mark 4 for 20–30 minutes, or until the top is crisp and golden brown.
2. Make a crunchy crumble by crushing a cup of cornflakes slightly and mixing with $\frac{1}{2}$ oz melted margarine. Add sugar and a teaspoon of golden syrup if the cornflakes are not sugar-coated. Sprinkle on the fruit and bake at 350°F/Gas Mark 4 for 15 minutes.

10 Drinks – Hot and Cold

HOT DRINKS

When you're feeling a bit low and not up to cooking, it is important to have something nourishing. At a time like this a hot milky drink is as good as a light meal and helps towards a good night's sleep. In the morning too, a good hot drink makes it easier to face dull winter days. Where the recipes use rum or whisky, it's worth while investing in a quarter bottle or a miniature.

Sweet Dreams Nightcap

½ pint warm milk
1 level dessertspoon clear honey
1 dessertspoon rum or whisky

Heat the milk and honey till boiling. Pour into a warmed glass. Stir in the rum or whisky. Drink at once.

Mocha Cuppa

1 cup of milk
2 rounded teaspoons drinking chocolate
1 level teaspoon instant coffee
Pinch of cinnamon
Sugar to taste
1 teaspoon cream (optional)
Grated chocolate (optional)

Bring the milk to the boil and stir in the drinking chocolate, instant coffee and a pinch of cinnamon and sugar to taste. Mix well. It's extra nice with a teaspoon of cream stirred in or with some grated chocolate sprinkled on top.

Mint Tea

Pour ½ pint of boiling water on to a teaspoon of dried mint and leave to infuse for 4 minutes. Strain and add a squeeze of lemon juice and sugar to taste. Good cold too.

Honey and Lemon

To the strained juice of a lemon add 1 dessertspoon of honey and ½ pint boiling water.

Treacle Posset

Put a tablespoon of golden syrup in a mug. Pour on boiling milk and stir well.

Sweet Vanilla Milk

Heat ½ pint milk and stir in 1 dessertspoon honey and 2–3 drops vanilla essence. Sprinkle a little cinnamon on top.

Mulled Ginger Tea

¼ pint hot tea
Thinly pared rind and juice of ½ orange
1 piece root ginger
Barbados sugar

Pour the tea over the orange rind and the bruised ginger (press the ginger firmly with a tablespoon). Leave to infuse for a few minutes. Strain into a mug or glass. Stir in the orange juice and a little Barbados sugar to taste.

Sailors' Saviour

Mix rum, a pinch of mixed spice, 1 dessertspoon of sugar and a knob of butter in a tumbler. Fill up with boiling water.

Whisky Cordial

Beat 1 egg yolk with a measure of whisky and a little sugar. Gradually pour on 1 cup of hot milk, beating all the time.

COLD DRINKS

Try some of these cold drinks on a hot summer's day. They make a change from the countless canned carbonated drinks on the market and are a lot better for you. Keep a jug of homemade real lemonade in the 'fridge or try some refeshing iced coffee instead of your usual hot morning drink.

Iced Coffee

Make some very strong coffee, allow it to cool and then chill it thoroughly. Put a little ice into a glass and pour in the coffee to come just over halfway up the glass. Fill the glass nearly to the top with very cold milk, then add a little thin cream on the top of the milk and sweeten to taste.

Vary by adding a spoonful of vanilla, coffee or chocolate ice cream or a spoonful of lightly whipped thick cream, sprinkled with grated chocolate.

Orange Egg Nog

Beat 1 small egg into ½ pint milk with 2 teaspoons frozen orange juice. Alternatively, whisk together ¼ pint canned orange juice with 1 small egg and a teaspoon of honey.

Prune Cream Soda

Beat 1 carton prune yogurt and ¼ pint milk together. Chill and serve topped with a spoonful of ice cream.

Egg Reviver

Beat up 1 egg well. Whisk in ¼ pint chilled tomato juice and a few drops of Worcester sauce. A refreshing pick-me-up, especially with some ice.

Tomato Juice Cocktail

Mix together ¼ pint tomato juice, 1 teaspoon sugar, 1 teaspoon lemon juice, ¼ teaspoon Worcester sauce and ¼ teaspoon salt. Chill and serve with an ice cube and a slice of lemon, if available.

Lemonade

Put the juice of 2 lemons, the grated or peeled rind of 1 lemon and 3–4 oz sugar in a jug. Pour on ¾ pint boiling water, cover and leave until cool. Strain, add another ½ pint cold water or soda water. Very refreshing.

Rose Cream Soda

1–2 tablespoons rose-hip syrup
1–2 tablespoons strawberry ice cream
½ small bottle soda water

Put the rose-hip syrup into a tall glass. Add the ice cream. Top with soda water and stir lightly.

Egg and Pineapple Flip

Beat together an egg yolk and ¼ pint canned pineapple juice. Stir in the stiffly beaten egg white. Pour into a glass and sprinkle with grated nutmeg if you happen to have some.

Iced Ginger Nog

Beat up 1 egg in a tumbler and add the strained juice of 1 small lemon and a little sugar. Fill up with iced ginger ale. Mix well.

Fruit Cup

Long fresh-fruit drinks are delicious and refreshing, and in summer any soft fruits, like raspberries and strawberries, can be quickly made into a fruit cup. (It's a good way of using up over-ripe fruit.) Mash the fruit with a little sugar (or, if a 'seedy' fruit, rub through a sieve) and add soda or plain water and ice.

Orange and Lemon Drink

Thinly slice 1 orange and 1 small lemon without peeling. Put the fruit slices in a jug, sprinkle over 1–2 tablespoons sugar and pour on 1 pint boiling water. Cover and leave until cool. Strain and serve as cold as possible.

11 Baking – Teatime Treats

Banana Bread

4 oz margarine or butter
8 oz castor sugar
2 eggs, lightly beaten
3 bananas, well mashed
8 oz plain flour
1 level teaspoon bicarbonate of soda

Cream the margarine or butter and sugar until light and fluffy. Gradually stir in the eggs and then the mashed banana. Sift the flour with the soda and a generous pinch of salt into a bowl, and stir into the banana mixture, a little at a time, until well blended. Turn into a well-greased loaf tin and bake at 350°F/Gas Mark 4 for 1¼ hours.

Serve hot or cold, sliced and buttered.

Honey and Milk Loaf

8 oz self-raising flour
4 oz butter
1 large egg
2 level tablespoons clear honey
3 tablespoons milk

Sift the flour into a bowl. Cut up the butter and rub into the flour until the mixture resembles breadcrumbs. Beat in the egg, honey and milk. Mix well. Turn into a greased 1-lb loaf tin and bake at 350°F/Gas Mark 4 for 1–1¼ hours.

Fruit Bread

8 oz self-raising flour
1 level teaspoon cream of tartar
1 level teaspoon bicarbonate of soda
1 teaspoon mixed spice
4 oz margarine
4 oz soft brown sugar
5 oz raisins, chopped
1 egg
½ pint milk

Sift the flour, cream of tartar, soda and spice. Cut up the margarine and rub into the flour. Stir in the sugar, egg, milk and raisins, and mix well. Bake in a greased tin at 325°F/Gas Mark 3 for 1 hour.

Foolproof Sponge Cake

Perfect every time.

3 eggs
6 oz castor sugar
2 oz butter
2 tablespoons water
4 oz self-raising flour

Beat the sugar and eggs until thick and creamy. Put the butter and water into a small pan and leave over a *low* heat until the butter melts (but don't let it boil). Stir into the egg mixture. Fold in the sifted flour and pour the mixture into two greased 7–8 inch sandwich tins. Bake at 375°F/Gas Mark 5 for 20 minutes. Turn out and leave to cool.

Fill with fruit or jam and a little whipped cream.

Scones

4 oz plain flour
1 oz butter, margarine or lard
¼ level teaspoon bicarbonate of soda
½ level teaspoon cream of tartar
¼ level teaspoon salt
4 tablespoons milk

Sift the flour, soda, cream of tartar and salt into a bowl. Rub in the butter, margarine or lard and mix to a soft dough with the milk. Turn on to a lightly floured board, knead lightly and roll out ½ inch thick. Cut into 2-inch rounds, using a small glass or cutter, and place on an ungreased baking tray. Brush over with a little milk and bake in a hot oven, 425°F/Gas Mark 7, for 10–15 minutes.

This quantity makes 6 scones.

If preferred, 1 level teaspoon baking powder can be used *instead* of the cream of tartar and soda.

Variations

1. Add 1 oz sultanas and a level tablespoon of castor sugar to the mixture before adding the milk.

2. Add 1½ oz finely grated cheese and a pinch of dry mustard to the mixture before adding the milk to make a savoury scone. These make good supper snacks, spread with butter and served hot with one of the following toppings:

(a) Tomato slices, anchovy fillets and black olives.
(b) Sliced hard-boiled egg and chopped green pepper.
(c) Stoned sliced dates and crisply fried bacon.
(d) Flaked canned salmon or tuna mixed with salad cream.
(e) Sardines mashed with a little vinegar and topped with chopped celery.

Biscuits

Basic biscuit mix

3 oz margarine or butter
3 oz castor sugar
1 egg
Milk
Flavouring – a few drops of vanilla, almond or lemon
  essence or ½ teaspoon ground cinammon
6 oz plain flour

Cream the margarine or butter and sugar until light and fluffy. Add the egg, flavouring and sifted flour. Mix well and add a little milk to make a pliable dough. Roll out ¼ inch thick on a board which has been lightly sprinkled with sugar, and cut into shapes. (The sugared board prevents the biscuits becoming tough.) Place on a greased baking tray and bake at 375°F/Gas Mark 5 for 10–15 minutes.

Variations

1. For spice biscuits – add ¼ teaspoon each of mixed spice and ground ginger to the flour when sifting.

2. Add a few chopped nuts, sultanas, currants or glacé cherries to the basic mixture.

12   Miscellaneous Hints

1. A few sugar lumps in the biscuit tin will help to keep the biscuits crisp.

2. Soak prunes in cold tea overnight, or orange juice (with a slice of lemon if you have one). Cook in the liquid for extra flavour.

3. Out of castor sugar? Crush granulated sugar with a rolling pin between two sheets of greaseproof paper.

4. If you have made scone dough too moist, don't stir in more flour. Sprinkle the baking tray with cornflour before cooking the scones.

5. A pastry cutter can be used for poaching eggs. Place the cutter in a pan of simmering water and drop in the egg.

6. Make up a batch of shortcrust pastry – i.e. rub fat into flour – and keep in a screw-top jar in refrigerator. Use for pastry by adding water; for crumble topping by adding sugar; or for white sauce by mixing with cold milk and bringing to the boil.

7. If honey goes sugary, stand the jar in a pan of hot water and the honey will liquidise again. If you're measuring honey or syrup, lightly grease or warm the cup, spoon or scale pan; this makes it much easier.

8. If you burn yourself, flood the burn with cold water. If it is very bad, hold a bag of ice cubes on the burn for 30 minutes.

9. A power-cut thought — candles will last longer and drip less if you put them into the refrigerator for a few hours before using.

10. To boil cracked eggs, wrap the egg tightly in foil or add vinegar to the water.

11. Cleaning pans — soak them as soon as you've finished cooking. If the pan has been used for flour mixtures, eggs or milk, soak it in *cold* water (hot water hardens the food). Soak fish dishes in cold water too, with a couple of drops of vinegar.

12. Rinse a pan in cold water *before* pouring milk in to heat; this stops the milk sticking to the pan.

Index